Praise for *Cello Notes*

Too often I hear: "I once played an instrument but regretfully I stopped long ago and now it is too late to start again." Mavis Himes proves that there is no age limit to further human creativity. *Cello Notes* provides great inspiration to those seeking deeper fulfillment through the arts. And it is worth it because, as Friedrich Schiller stated, "Only through art can we transcend the limitation of reality."

— **Cecylia Barczyk, concert cellist**

In *Cello Notes*, Mavis Himes probes her own late-stage embrace of the cello to create a universal statement on music as an illuminating, healing, and ecstatic pursuit. Himes writes with the insight of a therapist, the eye of a natural researcher, and the perseverance of a self-diagnosed overachiever. The reader joins her on a journey through triumphs and setbacks to arrive at greater appreciation of music's mysteries.

— **Alon Nashman, artistic director, Theaturtle**

In this touching and beautifully composed memoir about taking up the cello later in life, Mavis Himes explores the roadblocks and the breakthroughs that she experienced, the emotional highs and lows, the always present temptation to give up, and the transcendent joy to be found in persevering. Do dive into this masterly performance ... you will be so glad that you did.

— **Robin Elliott, Jean A. Chalmers Chair in Canadian Music, University of Toronto**

Cello Notes

Music and the Urgency of Time

Mavis Himes

Illustrations by Brian Gable

Published in 2024 by
Kinetics Design, KDbooks.ca
ISBN 978-1-998351-04-6 (paperback)
ISBN 978-1-998351-03-2 (ebook)

Edited by Michael Carroll
Cover and interior design, typesetting,
online publishing, and printing by Daniel Crack,
Kinetics Design, KDbooks.ca
www.linkedin.com/in/kdbooks/

Contact the author at mhimes@interlog.com

Cello Notes is a work of non-fiction, although a few
names and identifying features have been changed.

For Dobrochna and for all the magic-makers
of the world — old and young, named and unnamed.

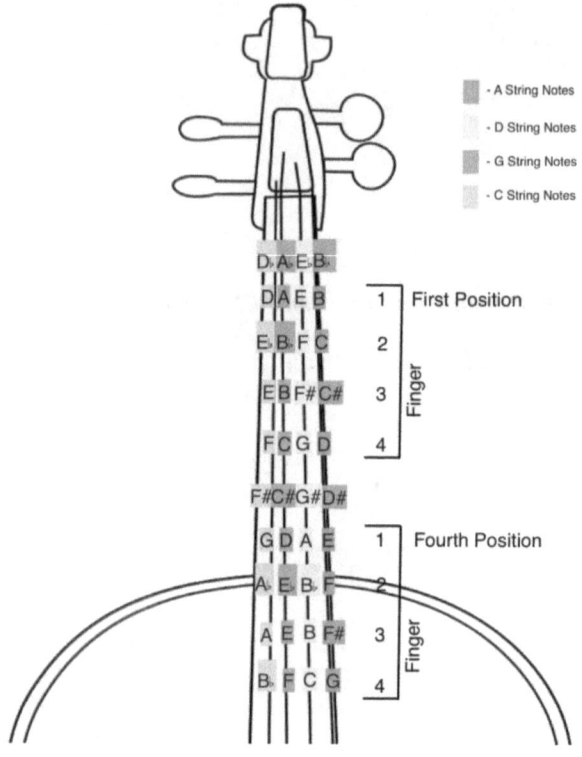

- A String Notes
- D String Notes
- G String Notes
- C String Notes

Dь Aь Eь Bь					
D A E B			1	First Position
Eь Bь F C			2	
E B F# C#			3	Finger
F C G D			4	
F# C# G# D#				
G D A E			1	Fourth Position
Aь Eь Bь F			2	
A E B F#			3	Finger
Bь F C G			4	

If the reader has already commenced the study of the 'cello, it will be advisable for either his parents or himself to make direct enquiries of his professor, whether the latter thinks the pupil is sufficiently gifted to continue the study of this most difficult instrument. Of course every 'cello player cannot be a Becker or a Klengel, but unless the student has a very correct ear, and if he is old enough a fair amount of ambition, it would be better for him to study some less exacting instrument; that is if he feels compelled to learn something.

— Arthur Broadley, *Chats to Cello Students*, 1899

Contents

Violon.

4.

Allegretto poco mosso.

dolce cantabile

pp

cresc

f

dim.

Prologue

That morning, I woke up hearing music in my head.

The fourth movement of César Franck's Sonata for Violin and Piano resonated deep within me, sending my spirit soaring. *I'm living music, just like my teacher Dobrochna Zubek and my hero Leonard Cohen. Just like Ludwig, Wolfgang, and the others.*

On that sunny summer day, I decided to bicycle downtown to meet my friend, Lois, at the launch of her new art show. Avoiding the major thoroughfare known to be a bowling alley for speeding cars, I chose an alternate route through a more residential area. At a three-way stop, a bus driver coming from the opposite direction waved me through a left turn.

And then it happened.

A clatter and a clash. A car door. An upended bicycle. A collision of metal and flesh.

Time halted in those few seconds in which I careened through space before hitting the middle of the road.

I didn't lose consciousness. I was surprisingly aware of my body's sudden plunge, the contact with something hard and permanent, the sound of my red bike smashing against the asphalt. I felt the thud of my limbs and the force of gravity.

I tried to orient myself to stand up but struggled and lay back down. I had landed with full force on my left side. My body ached but especially my arm. I couldn't move it to support myself in getting upright. I glanced over at my side and saw my elbow bone exposed like a fossil fragment in the sparkling sunshine. Out of the corner of my eye, a patch of red, not crimson or currant, but scarlet red, the colour of body sap, of fresh blood.

I'm alive, I'm alive, I'm still alive. Not music, but an echo resounded in my head. When I realized I hadn't sustained a life-threatening injury, my thoughts flew into an assortment of concerns: *I can't move my arm. Oh, shit, I had plans to work on the Bach minuet this month. Will I be able to play my cello again? What about my meeting with Lois?*

A male voice calmly interrupted my inner chatter. "Do you have your health card with you? Do you have someone I can call? We've already phoned for an emergency vehicle. They should be here momentarily."

I tried to focus on the questions directed at me. "What's your home number?" the voice asked. "Who can I contact?"

I believe I pointed to my shoulder pouch still strapped across my body. Succinctly, I enunciated the digits of my phone number as if my life depended on the clarity of each one.

Someone placed a phone by my ear and I heard my husband's voice. "Hello, hello? Is that you, Mave? Are you there? Is everything all right?"

Composed and in a state of hyper-serenity, I stated my location and what happened in brief staccato phrases: "An accident ... my arm ... I'm okay ... please come ..."

"I'll be there right away," I heard him say before someone removed the phone.

I put my head back down on the road.

Perhaps it was the same man with the calm voice who asked if I could stand in order to reposition myself off the street. I must have answered in the affirmative, even though my earlier attempt had failed, since a woman with an even softer voice helped me up and gently guided me onto the sidewalk. My left arm throbbed in revolt when I stood, and I realized I was holding it like an object. It wouldn't move of its own volition, nor could I will it to do so. While I couldn't see clearly without my glasses, I did know my arm was completely disconnected from my brain. I cradled the inert, unresponsive limb. Someone retrieved my glasses and placed them over my eyes.

Cadmium red. Yes, that's it! Cadmium red, that's the shade.

I lay on the sidewalk, and pointing to my saddlebag, asked for a sweater to shield my eyes from the glaring midday sun.

Within minutes, an ambulance and my husband both arrived.

"Will I be able to play the cello again?" I asked the medic as I was wheeled into the ambulance on a gurney.

Prélude

1

Taking Up the Cello

I first said it out loud to my mother in the spring of 2015. Massaging her feet as she lay on her bed with end-stage cancer, I announced, "Mom, I've decided to take up the cello." My ninety-one-year-old mother whose energy, youthfulness, and vitality I'd always admired, stared at me. Eighteen months earlier, she'd been diagnosed with stage four breast cancer metastasized to that part of the brain controlling balance and coordination. This third bout meant my mother was physically weaker but cognitively as astute and sharp as I'd always known her to be.

"Cello?" she said with a hint of doubt that betrayed her skepticism in my dedication to the task. "Did you say the cello? Did I hear right?"

"Yes, Mom, I've decided to learn the cello," I repeated, as if to confirm the integrity and conviction of my decision.

She glanced up from the plate of cookies atop her quilt, and with eyes wide and pupils dilated, she paused for a second before continuing. "Well, Mavis, you've always been full of surprises. And you always insist on following your own path wherever it leads. I wish you good luck on this new adventure."

I knew she was referring to past decisions I'd made, ones over which we'd fought and argued, both big and small. Such as the time I announced to my parents I was moving to Israel after resigning from my first job as a registered child psychologist.

"Why would you move to a country where you have to struggle when you have everything you could possibly want here? You always go against the current, Mavis."

I'd received a similar reaction of disbelief and awe from my mother when I told her I was going skydiving. "It's okay, Mom. I'll be doing a tandem jump, so I can double the height of a solo dive. No problem. I've already got a letter of permission from my doctor." And a few weeks later, I jumped out of an airplane at 10,000 feet near Lake Simcoe, north of Toronto.

For many years, combative interactions had certainly clouded the relationship I had with my mother. Both of us being stubborn individuals, we'd clashed over choices and decisions I made, my mother insisting on her rights as a parent to dictate my path forward, while I silently pursued my diversions without her knowledge or consent.

However, during the period of my mother's final illness, I spent most Saturdays taking her on outings that included lunch stops at her favourite Asian restaurants. And it was over bowls of steaming Vietnamese pho or Thai noodles that we mended our relationship.

"Do you remember when you forbid me to date J and I did it, anyway? Or do you recall when you told me not to see K because he wasn't Jewish? All that censure, all those rules. You were a tyrant, Mom! You could never just let me be and work it out for myself."

"You were always so impulsive. You always did what you wanted to in the end. So pig-headed, so stubborn and unreachable, you were."

Through the retellings of our entwined lives with mistaken facts and blurred memories, we restitched the shared canvas of our family history.

"Oh, yes," I said to my beautiful mother with the still-twinkling eyes and perfect skin, "your daughter's going to learn the cello. And you'll be able to hear my sounds wherever you are."

She smiled, and I reached over to hug her as cookie crumbs rolled onto the blanket.

I left that day and didn't mention another word about the cello to anyone. My life turned into a musical turntable of work and visits to that same apartment in the north end of the city while trying to conduct a normal routine with family and friends.

One night, four months after that first musical announcement, I received a phone call at 2:00 in the morning from the support worker who stayed with my mother overnights. The phone call I'd been anticipating for a while, the one that marked the end of an era for me and my sister, Linda. During the next days, Linda and I made the arrangements to mourn, honour, and eulogize our mother's life.

Perhaps it was the death of a second parent that made me take stock of my life more diligently. After all, I'd had finally reached a certain age and stage of life, that most unwelcome period of senior citizenship, a polite, euphemistic way of saying I was "getting old." Many of my friends and colleagues had already retired and were extolling the virtues of their decisions. They sent emails from various ports and cities around the globe, describing their strolls through the cobblestone laneways of Rome, wine tasting on the Danube, and hikes along the Camino de Santiago in Spain. Some attended "lifelong" university courses and lecture series, while others volunteered time at shelters or stuffed envelopes for local charities.

Like them, I, too, had been thinking about the possibility of retirement. I'd spent a lifetime working as a psychoanalyst, dabbling on the side with professional and literary writing. Admittedly, the prospect of unstructured time sounded both exciting and liberating, yet also left me with dread. I didn't feel ready to shred my clinical notes, pack up my textbooks on Lacanian and Freudian psychoanalysis, or empty my filing cabinet of the myriad articles I'd accumulated throughout the years. Recognizing my needs for intellectual and social stimulation, I wondered whether I could find enough satisfaction in retirement.

Perhaps it was this subterranean prattle, fermenting like some brew below my conscious awareness, that made me announce to my husband, Lawlor, three years after my mother's death, "I've decided to take up the cello." This time, I was more determined and available for such a pursuit. "I'm planning to find a teacher and purchase an instrument."

Lawlor, as always celebrating my decisions, replied, "That's wonderful!"

A deep impulse was propelling me to follow this interest. I knew the desire ran counter to the established literature on neurological growth, suggesting a juvenile brain was superior for the development of most cognitive and novel skills. Learning to play a new instrument would certainly fall into that category. And yet, I was determined to indulge in the pleasure and excitement of this challenge — blindly, bravely, boldly.

However, I sensed an urgency of time and knew I had to act quickly so as not to miss what seemed like a closing window of opportunity.

A crazy idea? A late-life crisis? Perhaps. But I was now ready to take on this endeavour with all the energy, passion, and commitment with which I'd approached all new interests. This time, the only thing I was less sure about was time's interference.

What if something happened to me, like Lawlor's completely unexpected open-heart surgery? What if I were to be diagnosed with something unforeseen myself? While my mother had lived a long and active life despite her temporary setbacks from three brushes with cancer, my father had died at the age of sixty-six after his third heart attack, a disease with a very strong genetic component in his family. And although I'd now surpassed my father's age, I didn't know how much more time the goddesses of fate would grant me.

I noticed myself and my friends becoming more attuned to the passage of time — the inevitability of its constant motion, its rhythm, its unfolding and uncoiling, its serpentine movement, and its lurching toward a personal finality.

"You know, Mavis," I remember my mother insisting, "enjoy your life now. Time passes so quickly."

As I grew up, her philosophy of *carpe diem* had always sounded hollow to my ears. Yet now, I wanted to embrace the present, determined to take advantage of whatever time I had.

So, being blessed with good physical health and ample energy, and forever grateful for the resources afforded me by my professional choice and lifestyle, I took the plunge into what became a startling new adventure.

2

My Teacher

*I*T was a blustery January afternoon in 2018 when I stepped into the overcrowded coffee shop at the edge of the University of Toronto's St. George Campus. Students in jeans and duffel coats hugged the walls and hoarded the stools and low chairs with their laptops propped upright.

I glanced around the room, not exactly sure how to identify the young woman who was to become my cello teacher. Dobrochna was the name I had, and the foggy memory of an accented voice, Polish, I thought. But I couldn't recall whether I'd revealed anything about myself. Perhaps I'd said, "I'll be the woman in the black coat with red gloves and a multicoloured scarf," or maybe I'd admitted I'd be the woman with tousled white hair, a few streaks of jet, and a patch of red near the neck.

As a member of the literary section of the Toronto Heliconian Club, a women's art association, I'd attended several of their musical concerts, literary salons, and visual art exhibitions. It was after an evening performance of her own compositions that I met Kye Marshall, a multi-talented cellist and composer. Months later, having finally committed to pursuing the cello myself, I enlisted her help in finding a teacher.

Without a moment's hesitation, Kye suggested a person she knew. "She's an excellent cellist, and I've just completed my opera and invited her to play the solo cello part. I'll send you her contact information."

Within a day, an email arrived in my inbox with a

Slavic-sounding name, Dobrochna Zubek, along with a phone number, website, and email address. A striking young woman stared out at me from her home page.

I immediately called Dobrochna, and we arranged a time and place to chat.

So there I was, mid-afternoon, at a university coffee shop awaiting our first meeting, feeling self-conscious about my age and how a "senior" student might appear to a younger woman. Would she have reservations about working with me? Is that why Kye had passed me on to someone else rather than taking me on herself? Would an accomplished performer and teacher want to invest time in someone who, in all likelihood, would never reach the potential measures of success awaiting a younger pupil? Perhaps, more significantly, I questioned whether she'd think me physically and mentally capable of mastering even the rudimentary skills required to play a string instrument. While I'd studied piano during childhood and adolescence, it was years since I'd looked at a sheet of music.

Arriving a few moments early, I shed my coat and studied the coffee menu above the counter. As I was about to place my order, I was approached by a tall woman with chestnut hair bundled up with a woolly scarf and hat. "Are you Mavis?" she asked, and before I was able to respond, held out her hand. "I'm Dobrochna. Pleased to meet you."

I glanced up at this woman with her outstretched hand already clasped in mine. A magnetic vitality and energy shone through her eyes, and I found myself immediately responding with an eager "Yes, I'm Mavis," matching her bold directness.

To this day, I'm not sure how she so confidently identified me from a roomful of strangers, but in time, I was to become familiar with her straightforwardness, which often translated into self-assuredness.

Dobrochna stood out as a study in lengths: long hair, long fingers, and long legs. On that day, a brightly coloured shawl was recklessly thrown around her neck and body atop a coat. As she removed her layers of warmth, I noticed her wrists were swaddled like precious babes in double-layered, hand-knitted wrist warmers. I admired the geometric pattern of red and black stripes interwoven with ivory buttons in the mini-shapes of a star, a seashell and an oblong treasure chest.

After settling into a high-top table amid the chaotic room, we placed our orders and returned to our seats. Awaiting our steaming coffee, we exchanged pleasantries.

Then, in an attempt to carry off the impossible task of being modestly boastful, I introduced myself through my professional accomplishments: my career as a psychoanalyst, my writings, my professional background. I mentioned my long-standing passion in dance, theatre, and music, as well as my patronage of multiple artistic events. I even revealed my early years of piano playing, confessing that my studies were disrupted when my musical and cultural pursuits were replaced with those of romance. For a moment, I felt as if I were performing at a job interview, trying to convince an interviewer, in this case, Dobrochna, why she should take me on as a student.

Imagining she might prefer to work with an aspiring and more malleable young cello student rather than a woman perhaps twice her age and reminiscent of an elderly aunt, I searched for more ammunition to win her over.

Aware of her Polish roots, I decided to engage in a ploy of "six degrees of separation" and asked, "Do you know Norbert Palej, the Polish composer and faculty member at the University of Toronto?"

"Yes, I do," she replied. "Very well."

Their close connection and friendship confirmed, I launched into talking about the work I'd done with Norbert on the intersection of psychoanalysis and the arts that culminated in a symposium I'd organized years earlier. When the conversation fell silent, I asked her to tell me about her own musical trajectory.

I learned she'd begun studying the cello at the age of seven in a Polish music school system that promoted general education in addition to the musical subjects normally covered in a conservatory program in Canada. "I was a bit late for serious virtuoso, you know. They start learning at age four," she added, laughing.

Briefly, she outlined the professional journey that had propelled her back and forth, criss-crossing the Atlantic on a migration from her home in Poland to the United States, from Mexico to Paris, and back again to Mexico. She said that after her studies with several well-known cellists, she decided to study with Shauna Rolston, an icon of Canadian cello talent, and complete her doctoral studies at the University of Toronto.

It wasn't long before Dobrochna turned to me and asked, in that direct way she had, "So tell, me, what is your desire with the cello?"

That word again, *desire*, the one that psychoanalysts were emboldened to ask.

I clammed up and choked out something about the lyricism, the melodious and mellow sounds and colours of the cello. I confessed how listening to certain string pieces moved me to tears and how I wanted to immerse myself in those sounds, maybe even create those same emotions in others.

The truth was I hadn't yet completely understood my own motivation for taking up this instrument. What I did know was that I was committed to discovering something about music and wished to pursue that desire as far as it would take me. I desperately wanted this first encounter to be the beginning of a prolonged journey. And I wanted my jitters at trying to establish a connection with this potential teacher to cease.

"And is there a piece of music you wish to play or master?" Dobrochna asked. "Something from the classical or contemporary repertoire?"

Again, my mind went blank. Was this a trick question

upon which her acceptance of me was to be determined? Did I have to come up with something immediately? "Well, I love the music of Leonard Cohen," I blurted, though I had no particular yearning to bastardize any of his songs with my playing.

"I could certainly provide you with an arrangement of one of his songs, if that's something you'd like to learn. It could be something to work toward."

Later, I'd admit that I really wanted to learn some of the standard repertoire for cello, such as Camille Saint-Saëns's *The Swan* or Max Bruch's *Kol Nidrei*, or the *Thaïs Méditation* by the French composer Jules Massenet, all very lyrical pieces that, for me, touched that elusive part of humans we call the soul. But that came much later after we'd been working together for some time.

We continued to talk about travel, since my husband and I were leaving on an African safari to Ngorongoro Conservation Area and Serengeti National Park in Tanzania for a few weeks. And then I heard the words I'd been so urgently awaiting. "Okay, then, Mavis, why don't we start when you get back from your trip? Maybe we can pin down a date in the first week of March."

My heart continued to pound as I reached for my calendar.

"Yes, and in the meantime, I think we should make arrangements for you to rent a cello."

"Of course, of course," I agreed with the enthusiasm of a child who had just won free access to a candy vault. "Shall we do that before or after I return?"

I no longer remember the conversation that ensued in that crowded and overheated coffee shop. What remained was the sense of a first step on a new journey and a rather tentative bond with an effervescent woman who was about to be my guide.

Upon returning from the burning beaches and sultry market-places of Zanzibar, I contacted Dobrochna immediately. She informed me she'd already checked out the possibility of adult-sized cello rentals and discovered none were available, since it was the middle of the academic year. Instead, she suggested we go to Geo. Heinl & Co. Limited, an instrument store she knew where I could purchase an inexpensive beginner cello and bow.

On another snowy day a month after my initial meeting with Dobrochna, I crossed the street from a parking lot, gave some change to a shivering man, and passed a variety store with three flowering orchids in the window. Climbing up five steps to a storefront on Church Street, I walked into the narrow room with wood-panelled flooring and investigated the backroom at what appeared to be an arcade of stringed instruments resting sentinel-like on stands.

I was told to have a seat until Dobrochna arrived and was shown a wingback chair with an endpin strap attached to a chair leg in front of a bay window. While waiting, I heard the stairs creak and turned to see a gentleman descend the stairs: a manicured look, soft and trimmed beard, and clear blue eyes with an apron over his wool dress pants.

"Is that Cabochard you're wearing?" he asked abstractly, as if addressing the room. "Are you the one filling this space with such a beautiful scent?"

It took a moment to realize the gentleman was directing this question at me. I sensed an air of familiarity.

"No," I responded innocently. Then, as if in a Proustian reverie, I was transported to the scene of my parents' bedroom where a glass bottle with a black velvet bow sat atop my mother's perfume tray. I could still smell the floral and musky scent of my mother's neck as she leaned over to kiss me good night.

"Oh," he said, as if disappointed. "I was sure it was you." And without skipping a beat, he asked if he could be of help.

When I informed him, I was waiting for Dobrochna, he strode off, leaving behind the trail of an unfinished conversation.

I was subsequently to learn that this enigmatic man was Ric Heinl, the current owner and grandson of George Heinl, Sr., whose moniker adorned the store he'd inherited. Geo. Heinl & Co. Limited was an atelier specializing in high-end string instruments.

Ric's pedigree was bred in the bone through his paternal line: his grandfather, George, apprenticed under his Uncle Johann, who manufactured violins in Schnecken, Austria. George went on to study at various shops in Vienna where he received a violin maker's diploma, then moved to London, England, to work. From there, he was sent to Toronto to head the violin department for R.S. Williams, the largest instrument manufacturer in Canada. Eventually, George opened his own Toronto atelier in 1926 as a master maker and supplier of string instruments and accessories. The store was passed on to Ric's father, Frank, and Uncle George, Jr., and finally, Ric and his brother, Russell, joined the family business. In 2003, after his father's death, Ric became the sole owner. George Heinl, Sr., made more than 150 instruments, patterned after the Stradivarius, Guarnerius, and Guadagnini models purchased and played by many world-renowned musicians.

"And what about your son?" I once asked Ric.

"Oh, he's chosen not to follow in the family footsteps. He's a successful graphic artist."

Upon Dobrochna's arrival, we were looked after by Andreas, the salesperson who himself had been a pianist, as well as long-standing member of what I came to know as the Heinl family. They began chatting and laughing like old school friends. While Dobrochna tried out different instruments, I sat back silently like a youngster observing her parents negotiate the purchase of her first "grown-up" accoutrement.

MAVIS HIMES

"Try this one and that one," she said, getting up from her seat and pointing to two instruments. "I like the sound of these two. See what you think."

"All right, sure," I agreed, exchanging seats with her.

I had absolutely no idea what I needed to hear or the ability to discriminate any differences in sound. The cellos felt awkward and bulky as I tried to wrap my arms around them. Without being offered a bow, I couldn't produce a sound but sat with my feet straddling either side of the endpin that extended to the floor.

Reflecting back, I could have bought absolutely anything that day but decided to put my trust in my teacher's recommendation when I sensed her preference for one over the other.

"I'll go with this one," I stated emphatically, as if to demonstrate a certain level of feigned competence.

Then Dobrochna tested several bows. "Now try these different bows. One's wood and one's carbon fibre. See which feels better in your hand. Consider the weight of each of them and see if one's more comfortable for you."

In the end, I chose the carbon fibre bow, which seemed marginally lighter. But it might have been the colour that drew me to it, or that my teacher appeared to think it matched the cello better.

A few accessories were added to the purchase: rosin for the bow, a cello case, an endpin strap, and a small vial of cello oil.

"Now you're all set, my dear," Dobrochna told me. "We're ready to start playing the cello." She smiled as we exited the store, crossed the street, and loaded my new purchases into the back of my car. "You'll have to come up with a name for your cello," she added. "All cellists assign their instruments personal names. Take your time and it'll come to you."

3

First Lessons

On a late-afternoon in March 2018, Dobrochna and I agreed to meet on the St. George Campus of the University of Toronto at the chapel of Knox College. Limited by time, I decided to drive the few blocks from my office to the majestic and dignified limestone Christian theological school and seminary of the Presbyterian Church of Canada.

Walking up the outside entrance through the courtyard, my cello awkwardly strapped to my back, I heard my boots click on the tile flooring with a resounding echo, making me momentarily self-conscious. A feeling of exaltation overtook me as I entered the main building with its cathedral-like solemnity. Behind a partition of glass, a young student pointed me in the direction of the chapel. I slowly mounted the stairs with a feeling of divine ascension.

As I entered the room, I was reminded of the great Old World cathedrals — the Duomo in Venice and Notre Dame in Paris. Dwarfed by the height of the vaulted ceilings and the elegant stained-glass windows, I was tempted to sit piously in one of the wooden pews in gratitude and meditation. This hallowed place was to be the space for my musical beginning, my first step on what I dreamt to be a musical ascension.

I sat on one of the benches and listened to a violin and piano duet rehearsing a Vivaldi sonata while I waited for Dobrochna to arrive. Suddenly, I heard the opening of the chapel door and turned to see my teacher flying in from the cold.

She strode over to me, waving her hand. "Here, let's go over there," she said, leading me to a side corner up a few stairs. "There's better lighting here and a table we can use." As we settled into the space, she helped me unpack my cello case and demonstrated the preliminary setup of the instrument.

Following instructions, I'd come prepared with my *Suzuki Cello Book 1*, a tried-and-true successful primer for beginners of the cello. At the back of each book, numbered 1 to 10, is the picture of a student holding a cello. In *Book 1*, it's the waist shot of a little girl with blond bangs and hair tied in a ponytail, smiling at the photographer. Her hands are curled around the neck of the cello, which has white tape placed in equal intervals around it. I stared at the multiple images of this girl with her various hand placements.

Where was she now, I wondered. Who was this girl? Did she become a musician? Would I recognize her name today as a performer? Was she some kind of child prodigy? Were her parents musicians and did they force her to study the cello?

At the beginning of each Suzuki volume is an introduction to the student, the teacher, and the parents, outlining their respective roles and obligations. I was reassured to read that "musical ability is not an inborn talent but an ability that can be developed" and that "all children who are properly trained can develop musical ability just as all children develop the ability to speak their mother tongue."

Naturally, I wondered about older adults who decided to play music. Could we also develop this musical ability? Or were we more like awkward and dyslexic children trying to learn a second or third language? Had I missed a critical period of learning? Was it only children who could develop this so-called "musical ability"?

In the front of the book, I noticed another photograph of

an orchestra of children playing cellos, their heads bowed forward in unison as they pull their bows across the strings, their fingers uniformly placed. *Where, oh, where, is there a place for me in this ensemble of youngsters?* I lamented.

After getting me comfortable behind the cello, Dobrochna led me through an introduction of the basics: a description of the cello and its various parts; the correct body posture while sitting, torso upright with weight balanced equally on both buttock cheeks near the front of the chair; the setting up of the endpin, the pointed metal at the base that held the cello in a fixed place with a pin guard; the left-hand position, in the shape of the letter *C*, on the neck of the cello; the right-hand position on the bow, also cupped like the letter *C*; and the names of the four strings in descending order from left to right — A, D, G, and C.

I was encouraged to begin pressing down on the fingerboard with my left hand while sliding the bow across the strings with my right. My first attempts produced something of a sound, not a screech but neither a recognizable musical note. I tried a few more times and finally a clear sound emerged and stretched out. I smiled inwardly at my achievement.

Dobrochna told me that the arms and hands had to work independently of each other, and that I must practise in front of a mirror to observe what my right and left hands were doing. She demonstrated on her own cello various basics she wished me to imitate. The richness of sound in her playing of simple exercises took on the dimension of a recital performance within the acoustical vault of the Knox chapel. I wanted to just listen to her perform for me.

MAVIS HIMES

"Twinkle, Twinkle, Little Star," so universally embedded in the Western musical canon, has become one of the first tunes most string instrumentalists learn. With its inscribed simplicity and familiarity, any deviation, missed note, or incorrect intonation could be detected. And so "Twinkle, Twinkle" was the first piece of music I learned, too.

Written out on a piece of paper, in an elementary format, I was initiated into the beginner's world of cello playing with this popular tune as follows:

```
00 00 11 0
DD AA A —
44 33 11 0
D ——————————
```

And on and on ...

Within this matrix, the numbers indicated the fingering of the left hand, 0 representing an open string whereby no pressure was applied in the left hand, each subsequent number denoting the finger to be pressed on the fingerboard. The letters designated the string to be played. "Twinkle, Twinkle" was only played on the first two strings (A and D) throughout the piece.

And yet, how to put into words the elation and sense of mastery when I performed these few lines unfettered by tense shoulders and awkward fingers? It was like riding a bicycle for the first time without the training wheels.

Initially, I learned to play through the tune in a simple format. Later, I achieved it in all its bowing variations and dynamics: *pizzicato* ("plucking"), *arco* or *legato* ("smoothly"), *allegro* ("briskly"), *lento* or *largo* ("slowly"), *piano* ("softly"), or *forte* ("loudly"), culminating later with *vibrato* ("pitch variation").

Overwhelmed by the volume of information acquired that first day, I pulled out some loose paper and fastidiously noted everything I could recapture after the lesson.

"You know, Mavis, it will be a good idea for you to buy a journal and record the lesson notes each week. That way you'll have an overview and reference point for our work together."

I vigorously nodded and thought: *Words of wisdom. I should have already known this. I'll be prepared for the next lesson.*

As I write now, I reread those first introductory lessons and chuckle:

Open strings are the notes we play without needing to press any of the strings. Place and take off your finger in a timely rhythm on every string. Keep your hand in an open position. Position the thumb on your left hand under the second finger. Adjust your elbow to each string, raising slightly as you move across the strings.

On the way home from my first lesson, I grinned at the seeming paradox of my indoctrination into the world of the cello with "Twinkle, Twinkle" played in the chapel of Knox College. I wondered what the angels would think of my sounds in that space filled with grandeur and solemnity. If only I could have played a Bach cello suite.

In the privacy of my own space at home, I placed my bow on the cello and slid it across the strings. I no longer remember the awkward and dissonant sounds I made in those first few weeks. Dobrochna had encouraged me to sit in front of a mirror and told me to relax and breathe. She also advised me to execute some finger, wrist, and hand warm-up exercises in preparation for the demands to be made on my body.

I tried to comply as best I could, yet the cello always felt awkward and bulky. My exercises became coded in a new lexicon: "Tip to bow and bow to tip. Horizontal gate, vertical gate, and merry-go-round. Around the world with wrist. Imaginary tunes with a pencil. Walking like a leapfrog up and down the bow."

For those not familiar with the cello's physical details, a mini-lesson: unlike a guitar, the classical string family of instruments (violin, viola, cello, and base) have no frets, the small, raised metal bars across the neck to indicate finger placement required to produce different notes — a nightmare for beginner students. Under Dobrochna's directive, I placed tape on the neck of my cello to mark these finger placements in first position, starting with white adhesive strips, since I couldn't find anything else appropriate. Subsequently, I chose green masking tape and carefully replaced the bands of winter white to springtime.

I became addicted to the tape for finger placement. I couldn't start a piece or play a scale without lining my fingers up along the strips. How would I ever play without my beginner's tape? How would I ever manage to know where to place my fingers, where the notes were?

During that first year, my lessons alternated between the Knox chapel and the overcrowded practice rooms of the university's music faculty. It was Ping-Pong between the sacred and the profane as these latter rooms typically reverberated with the vibrato of a soprano doing warm-ups or the repetitive scales of a student pianist. Without adequate soundproofing, music leaked between rehearsal rooms and provided no privacy. I became accustomed to the search for a cello stand, a stool, or an adequate lamp at the start of each class held there.

Within a few weeks, I mastered the most rudimentary skills of my instrument: hand, wrist, elbow, and shoulder placements and integration; attention to different muscle groups; tension and release; and an appreciation of anatomically neutral positions. My challenge was learning to avoid drowning in an ocean of new information: scales, chords, the correct spinal position while seated; a dynamic technique that adopted different positions and angles of the body, arms, and hands, depending on what one was playing; the employment of multiple sets of muscles for a particular task; a glossary of Italian musical terms for tempo and dynamics; and musical theory and repertoire and composers.

Some days I left lessons feeling secure in my mastery of a technical move or conquest of a musical passage. My *Suzuki Book 1* introduced me to simple folk songs — "French Folk Song," "Song of the Wind," "May Song" — all of which consisted of three or four lines of music annotated with fingerings above each note, in addition to the dots and lines indicating the direction of the bowings (**⊓** for down bow and **V** for up bow) and dynamics. In those first months, Dobrochna also added letters of the strings to be played under the staff.

"I'm learning to play by numbers," I complained, both comforted and distressed by the numberings. I knew they were necessary as an *aide-mémoire* without which my brain would be overwhelmed, yet wishing I could move beyond the primers reminiscent of paint-by-number colouring books.

As the *Suzuki* volume progresses, folk tunes are replaced by short melodies of Shinichi Suzuki himself, the founder and educator of the method bearing his name and who lived to be 100 years old. Finally, by the end of that first year, I was playing a Robert Schumann song, a Bach minuet in C, and another Bach minuet, No. 2, tunes that most people would likely recognize. The final piece, Henry Purcell's *Rigadoon*, I later performed for a group of friends.

Typically, I required two to four weeks to learn the notes of a piece and for both my left and right hands to master their parts. For more challenging pieces, I was encouraged to play each hand separately before doing them together. Dobrochna slowly and patiently listened to my playing as I gripped my fingers on the neck of the cello and gritted my teeth. Despite her encouragement, I wasn't convinced about the mini-steps I was making and regressed to the tactics of a child trying to impress her teacher. "I know I played this one better when I practised alone in my room. Just me and my cello."

Dobrochna smiled. "I'm sure you did. That's the way it goes."

The more pressure I felt, the worse my playing, which resulted in frustration after my lesson. I was determined to improve in my next attempt. I practised consistently and diligently to meet my mini-goals, yet at the next lesson, I was once again bombarded by a new onslaught of fresh "learning tips."

"You know, it never stops," Dobrochna said when I complained about my impatience with the process, "because we can *always* improve and there's *always* something else to learn. You know that yourself, Mavis. I'm not saying anything you haven't already heard."

Of course, she was right, but to be confronted with the slow pace of success, especially at my age wasn't only humbling, it was irksome. I tried to convince myself the steeper the learning curve, the more satisfying the victory of mastery.

Of course, my first music books were laced with comments — pencilled ones such as "great job!" and smiley faces. I lapped up whatever positive feedback I received. Dobrochna had already forewarned me she wasn't an effusive giver of compliments and that the greatest accolade would eventually come from an appreciation of my own progress.

One day, my teacher brought in a manilla envelope, and at the end of the lesson, opened it and held out her hand. "Well, which is your favourite?" she asked, fanning out a deck of stickers packages — birds, animals, stars, and flowers.

When I chose a sheet of birds, she selected a sticker and placed it on "The Happy Farmer" by Schumann.

MAVIS HIMES

"I've decided to call my cello Daisy," I announced at my next lesson. "The name just appeared to me one morning and I liked the sound and timbre of it."

"Great!" Dobrochna said.

The lesson proceeded with constant hesitations and faltering in my playing. Not surprisingly, I received no stickers that day. Returning home, I scowled at the door.

"I guess it didn't go so well?" Lawlor said in a combined intonation of question and statement. "Remember *Zen Mind, Beginner's Mind?*"

Without responding, I slumped onto the sofa.

Lawlor was reminding me of lessons from his favourite book on Zen Buddhism, written by a Zen master in the early 1970s. "Remember its central message?" he asked, waiting for me to respond.

I said nothing.

"Anything's possible with a beginner's mind," he added.

I glanced up, filled with ire, like a balloon about to burst. "Really?" I was seething while fully aware of the truth to which Lawlor was alluding. What did all beginners have in common? Curiosity and enthusiasm, creativity and excitement. The frisson of new ventures that invited endless possibilities and opportunities.

New beginnings contained promises of freshness and growth, I told myself. Beginnings recalled the deeply embedded memories of *firsts*. First day of school, first overnight sleepover, first cigarette, first ski run down a slalom course, first kiss. My list of firsts had grown exponentially over the years, always accompanied by the exhilaration of novelty and newness, the elation of success.

Of course, I can do this, I thought. *I'm determined and challenged to take on the world. Well, maybe just the cello.*

I quickly realized my new endeavour involved a total engagement of both body and mind, and I couldn't pretend or try to fool Daisy with half measures. Her unforgiving clamour for attention and commitment reminded me of a jealous lover's command. Not only was she taking control, demanding complete subservience and surrender to her bidding, but she was asking me to change my body shape. My torso and limbs were required to stretch and shift in ways they'd never known. I'd become a corporeal multi-tasker.

Your hands and arms are to operate independently of each other. The weight of your hands must come from the larger muscle groups of your shoulder and elbow.

Every lesson involved the regurgitation of the same principles with new ones added.

Your left arm is to be fixated on placing pressure on the strings — A, D, G, C. Now create a C-shaped position with your left hand, your thumb between the second and third fingers. A simple C. You might want to practise wrapping your hands around a tennis ball, no, perhaps a squishy ball. You'll have to find the right-sized ball for your hand.

I positioned my hand as requested.

Now try to relax. Relax your fingers.

How do I relax my fingers while trying to apply pressure? How do I drop my thumb loosely while strengthening the rest of my fingers? My hand was too loose, my fingers too tight. I paced the living room, my hand cupped around the ball treasured by Gypsy, our beloved labradoodle.

"She'd be honoured to know you're using her toy," Lawlor said. "She'd love it."

"No, she'd be jealous and start barking for it," I countered argumentatively. While my left hand was struggling with the letter *C*, my right hand was learning the correct position for bow holding.

Yes, another C, but not the same one.

"Of course not," I muttered under my breath.

Here your fingers need to rest gently on the front of the bow and you must arc your thumb underneath.

I was cursed with my grandfather's hands — veiny and thin-skinned. When I was twenty, a man in an antique store asked me if I lived in the country. Quizzically, I stared at him and shook my head. "You have the hands of a working woman who lives on a farm," he told me.

I wrapped my wizened hands around the bow, holding my breath as I tried to adapt to the correct position. The task appeared impossible. I couldn't accommodate my long fingers to the bow's form. They wouldn't gently slide down and over the side of this baton-like stick with its strands of horsehair.

When held correctly, it created a sound that miraculously filled the universe. But my fingers felt too long and drooped over the side without control. No matter how many manual warm-up exercises I tried, my hand refused to co-operate. I wanted to cry from frustration.

Pasted above my desk at home is a quote by the Russian novelist Vasily Grossman from his novel *Stalingrad*: "You can write down the words of a song. You can describe the singer, the melody and the look in the listeners' eyes. You can write about the listeners' sorrows and longings — but will all this conjure a song into being? A song that makes people weep? Of course not. How could it?"

I persisted because I wanted to make people weep with the beauty of my cello playing, in the same way my body tingled when I heard "Au fond du temple saint" by Georges Bizet, more commonly known as "The Pearl Fishers' Duet."

Eventually, I told myself, I'd learn how to manage these impossible positions, but my muscles and bones, tendons and ligaments, all needed to develop into a symphonic paradigm that worked in harmony. Yes, I'd master how to make the elbow follow the hand and how to involve the whole weight of my arm and shoulder in this process. Yes, I'd comprehend the correct arm position and placement for each string.

Once again, in a different phrasing, I heard, as if from Daisy herself: *Your hands are separate. They work independently of each other, but they also work together as they both share the music. You must focus first on one and then on the other. Now place your bow on the string. Check your bow hold and pronate your hand. Make sure the bow is parallel to the bridge. Go from position to location. Down to the right and up to the left.*

Everything felt counterintuitive. As I moved my hand down on the neck of the cello, I was going higher in pitch, while coming back up I was lowering it. Down bow was to the right, up bow to the left.

I wasn't learning one language, I told my friends. I was discovering a Tower of Babel with competing voices and accents.

One day, my friend, Rhona, mentioned a mutual colleague, Liz, who I hadn't seen in many years. She, too, had decided to study the cello before her retirement. However, Rhona informed me that Liz had retreated from her musical studies.

I needed some reassurance, so I decided to call Liz and ask her about her experience with the cello. She was full of praise and wonder for the musical magic she'd experienced while playing. She mentioned she'd even joined an amateur orchestra and found that to be the most rewarding part of her cello journey.

"But I gave it up because I found my instrument way too arduous to lug around on my back. You know, I don't drive, so I began having back issues with all my toing and froing," she explained.

I tried to imagine this petite woman manoeuvring on buses and subways, walking down streets in a rush to get to a lesson or a performance practice. I was to have a similar experience when my car needed repair and I navigated the city with the cello on my back. While I enjoyed the smiles I received from fellow musicians — or so I imagined them to be — it was certainly onerous navigating long distances.

About to hang up the phone, I remembered to ask Liz,

MAVIS HIMES

"And what about the tape? When did you or your teacher decide you could try playing without it?"

Silence ensued on the other end of the line, and then a question. "What tape?" Another long pause. "I never had any tape on my cello."

"Thanks, Liz," I said quietly, then terminated the call.

I stared at the picture of the five-year-old girl smiling at the camera with her straight hair, bangs, and white teeth. She was holding a cello with strips of tape placed on the precise positions of the first, third, and fourth fingers: *Suzuki Book 1*.

Yes, I was an absolute beginner.

4

Relationships

Some new relationships begin slowly, cautiously, tentatively; others start with the shadow of an ending cast from the first moment: an excited approach, a pause, an expeditious retreat. My relationship with J began *subito, presto*. An adventure on wheels, a motorcycle ride that thrilled me for months before it collided with the reality of an alcohol addiction leading to total wreckage. My relationship with S was the opposite. A slow waltz of seduction *dolce, largo* like the unfolding of blooms in spring. We embraced, slid against each other, and tried desperately to explore the notes and rhythms of each other's body. My relationship with C was *agitato* and *giocoso*. We laughed and cried over movies by François Truffaut and Bernardo Bertolucci, Federico Fellini and Roman Polanski. We avoided any topics or conversations that disturbed the lightness of our beings. And in the end, we drifted apart, still laughing and crying about life's fanciful tragedies.

My relationship with Lawlor, who was to become my eternal soulmate, began *dolce, espressivo*, but *sempre sostenuto*. We walked the boardwalk along the shores of Lake Ontario under frosty December skies while the rest of the world lay sleeping. We roamed through cobblestoned ways of Etruscan and Roman kings, dived into the Dead Sea like giant balloons floating on the water's surface. Our relationship blossomed, matured, and has endured over the decades.

Recalling my past relationships made me reflect about my

newly minted one with Daisy, which had begun *poco a poco, adagio*. While we played together every day, my approach was cautious and hesitating. Daisy's body was hard and resistant, not porous and soft. At first I tried to familiarize myself with her wooden body, which was still unyielding and initially unwieldy. She was bulky in a way that felt alien. And yet, I had to adapt to her shape to create the sound I wished to produce.

I embraced her with limbs wide and torso taut. I enclosed my knees against the ribs of her middle and opened my feet outspread to land equidistantly on either side of her endpin. Raising my arm, I placed it on the fingerboard, fingers firmly hanging from the strings. None of this felt natural or comfortable. It took months to become settled and comfortable with this awkward position, let alone become familiar in this developing relationship. I was convinced it would take years to establish any bond of ease without the interference of physical constraint.

Once again, I remembered Dobrochna's words on my first day: "You have to imagine yourself playing the cello. You must be able to visualize yourself with your instrument."

"I'm not sure I can do that," I replied the first time I'd heard those words.

"It will take time." Dobrochna paused, and added, "No, it will take a lifetime."

But what if I don't have enough time? What's a lifetime for me now?

Early on in my lessons, I took out a subscription to *The Strad*, a glossy British magazine for musicians with feature articles on music and musicians, on lutherie, on teaching and learning, and on recording reviews. That meant each month I could anticipate the arrival of its monthly issue. That said, due to typical obstructions in the Canadian postal system, the delivery of my first copy arrived two months late in what became a recurring pattern.

In one of the *Strad* issues I received, a particular article immediately caught my attention: "In response to readers' letters, violin pedagogue Alvin C. White tackles the difficult subject of when — if ever — someone might become too old to learn the violin." White writes that late beginners always question whether they're too old to learn: "He feels that he will be slow at comprehending, that his fingers will be too stiff and although he does not say so, he inwardly feels that others will think he is a fool to start to learn to play at his age."

I was reassured to read that prospective students or lovers of music should never let age deter them from playing an instrument. With even more conviction, White adds that older pupils can be even "quicker at grasping an idea than many a younger one." He then proceeds to describe the range of students he's taught, always discovering within them a drive and determination that propelled them in their playing. He concludes: "One of the greatest drawbacks to the older prospective pupil is the feeling of humiliation in learning to play an instrument at his age, and the thoughts others may be thinking of him." As I came to the end of the article in which there was no mention of any age limit, I was relieved to read that White's oldest student was seventy-eight, and that he credited her with the advantage of being retired with lots of time to practise.[1]

A hopefulness and calm overtook me as I moved into my day. I considered all the positive effects of cello playing in addition to the pure pleasure: a calisthenic workout for my grey matter that, according to my readings, was bound to increase my concentration and attention, reward me with more focus, and improve my mood regulation. Neuroscientists agreed that later-life learning added benefits not only to neural expansion and development but quality of life. I was prepared to realize all these advantages.

As usual, I ended my lesson that day, placing Daisy in her case and then into the back seat of my car. I thought about her as a person and promised her that she'd become a part of my daily life and that one day we'd make great music together, committed to putting in the time and energy required for that to occur.

I felt utterly foolish talking out loud to Daisy as I pulled up to a red light. "You know, Daisy, it might start with 'Twinkle, Twinkle,' but one day it'll be Edward Elgar's Opus 85 or Johann Sebastian Bach's Cello Suite No. 6."

After four months, Dobrochna announced she was going home to Poland for four weeks in the summer. "A bit of work and a bit of pleasure," she declared.

I was caught completely off guard. "But, but … you can't leave now!" I stammered, trying to conceal my feeling of being dropped. "Just as I was beginning to feel so comfortable. We've become so tight, so close. What will I do when you're gone?" I knew I must have sounded like a child whose parents were about to go off on a vacation. The truth was I'd developed a strong attachment to both my instrument and my teacher. My reaction certainly testified to the strength and commitment of those bonds.

Despite the similarities to the complex and dynamic relationship that occurred so spontaneously in my work as an analyst, I hadn't anticipated my teacher's departure triggering such a response in me. "I can't believe I'm having this reaction to your holidays, Dobrochna. It's like that well-known phenomenon in psychoanalysis when analysts go on vacation. You know, like in Judith Rossner's novel *August*? But seriously, what will happen with my playing over the month you'll be away? I'll lose all my gains just as I'm getting started."

"No worries," she replied with calm reassurance. "I'll

hook you up with one of my colleagues. I've already thought about this and have two teachers in mind. Let me see who's available, and whoever it is, I'll share your learning history and what I'd like the substitute teacher to develop with you."

Relief settled in as we resumed my lesson.

Two months later, I presented myself at the door of a small bungalow in the east end of the city. I rang the doorbell and waited nervously for someone to appear. A rather short woman with brown hair and nondescript features welcomed me in. She smiled and asked me to have a seat on the stool in the front room. After a few introductory comments and informal chitchat, we settled into the lesson.

What occurred during the lesson was somewhat of a blur. I suspect it began with what I heard as a stringent command regarding my finger placement. I attempted to explain that I hadn't been taught what was being asked of me, but my words appeared to land flat. I felt I was being reprimanded for being a disobedient child. From that moment on, I became paralyzed in my playing, feeling light-headed and disoriented. I tried to muddle my way through the rest of the lesson, but the damage had already been done. A talented musician had reduced me to a shaking leaf.

I tried to make the most of the remaining time of the lesson, and at the end, this teacher asked if I wished to schedule another lesson. Trying to be polite and hiding my emotions, I told her I'd think about it and let her know. Then I heaved my cello onto my back and made a hasty exit.

That night I texted a friend: "Cello appears to be turning me into a child. I'm regressing rapidly and may need a few therapy sessions!"

The following day, I emailed Dobrochna and suggested we have a Skype call to discuss my lessons. As soon as I heard her voice, I exploded with words like *destroyed* and *devastated* to describe my experience with a teacher supposedly well versed in working with adult students.

Dobrochna was apologetic but didn't quite understand the depth of my disappointment and dispiritedness. In a very matter-of-fact tone, she informed me, "I'll arrange for you to see Brenton. He's very different, and I'm sure you'll like him. Mavis, please don't fret or stay upset. This happens sometimes. We never know with whom we can work. Sometimes we try and it doesn't pan out, so we try someone else. We'll be sure to alleviate this problem. Not to worry." Her voice of calm and reason settled my turbulent mind.

In retrospect, I recognize the substitute teacher's comment hadn't been a direct criticism but a correction, an attempt at a technical modification. She'd simply asked me to do something of common practice that Dobrochna hadn't insisted on yet. Later, I learned that Dobrochna had her own reasons for waiting to bring my attention to that particular finger placement, which had to do with muscle readiness.

A couple of days later, I received an email from Brenton requesting me to contact him for a lesson time. The following Monday, a young man with jet-black hair tied neatly in a ponytail arrived at my door. Dressed in cut-off shorts, black T-shirt embossed with a white Puma logo, and flip-flop sandals, he extended his hand as the weight of a cello case strapped to his narrow frame propelled him forward.

"Hi, I'm Brenton," he said breathlessly as he strode through the front door. "Sorry, I'm a few minutes late. Parking. Your street has few parking spaces, so I had to drive around the block and then cross the main street over there before I could find a spot. And then I had to bring my girl," he added, gently patting his decal-decorated case.

"Come in. Welcome, Brenton," I said, feeling immediately at ease with his youthful and buoyant energy.

At the end of our first lesson, a ninety-minute marathon, I was exhausted.

"I guess that was a bit too much," he said, observing my frazzled state.

A full day of work followed by such intense concentration outpaced my capacity to stay on track. I was certainly not as young and energetic as I used to be. Over time, however, I became accustomed to Brenton's disinhibited speech and verbal outpourings, though he'd still overwhelm me with a barrage of information and tips.

Our student-teacher relationship was comfortable and satisfying. I appreciated his intense zeal and desire to impart as much guidance as possible. Despite his casual attire and carefree manner, Brenton turned out to be stricter and more demanding than Dobrochna in his directives, always insisting on specific technical manoeuvres.

"Now, Mavis," he'd say, "I know you can do better than that. When you practise, try just going from one note to the next, bar by bar, until you get it correctly." Or "Maybe you should try the music app on your cellphone, the one that includes a metronome. That way you can become familiar with the phrasing, then increase or decrease your tempo as you see fit."

I shuddered remembering my first piano teacher, Mrs. Petrovsky, whose strict precision in timing had always intimidated me. "It's all right, Brenton. I think I'll just try to focus on intonation for now," I countered.

Or he'd say, "Mavis," with a hint of irritation in his voice, "you need to remember to keep your third finger down with your fourth finger for support and strength. That'll help you produce a fuller sound. Besides, why wouldn't you want to take advantage of this placement so you can be prepared for the next bar?"

My fingers still rebelled against the awkward positions and the unfamiliar extensions, but I persisted under his guidance.

"You know, when I speak to my young students," he said one time, and I pictured a row of little chicks all neatly lined up, "I tell them to make the fuck sign like this in order to go for it." He demonstrated opening his fingers one by one from a fist and holding up his middle finger tall as a tower. "They all chuckle. So go for it, Mavis. Just let your fingers open as wide as possible. Maybe Dobrochna gave you some exercises for that. I can suggest some to her if she didn't."

In comparison, I recognized Dobrochna's more organic approach with me. She tailored her teaching to my particular personality, my advanced years, my body, my fingers, always trying to match me with my cello. Aware of the inflexibility and perhaps limitations of a more mature body with less elasticity, Dobrochna encouraged the gradual strengthening and stretching of my fingers and hands, the measured extension of my arms and release of my shoulders in a safe manner without the imposition of too stringent dictates on my upper body. And very steadily, my body adapted to the new claims being made.

However, I also became fond of Brenton's manner and style and appreciated the value of his advice and suggestions. When it was time for our last lesson, we hugged and promised to keep in touch.

My sessions with Dobrochna resumed in the fall. I fell into her arms with gratitude upon her return. Brenton's teaching had left me with a list of new rules written in my homework book.

Dobrochna noticed slight improvements as she added more technical elements to my growing repertoire: string crossing using the infinity sign as an image, varying the speed of my scales; weight transfer in my fingers with attention to my thumb position; navigating with my elbow;

anticipation in my left hand. New information never ceased from lesson to lesson.

As I closed my eyes to hear the sound of my playing, I imagined myself in a canoe when I played "Lightly Row" or crooning to an old beau when I switched to "Song of the Wind."

I was encouraged to learn my pieces in small chunks, bar by bar or two bars by two bars, then line by line. She also encouraged me to memorize pieces so that I could more easily sink into the dynamics and musicality of the piece and shift my focus off technique.

Insisting I couldn't memorize any of the pieces, I told Dobrochna they demanded too much of my brain power. As ammunition, I reminded her of a master class I'd watched with cellist Mischa Maisky and students at the Jurmala Academy in his hometown of Riga, Latvia. With his wild mane of white hair and gold necklaces, Maisky displayed his flamboyant personality in his teaching, which exuded the confidence with which he's still celebrated. Having studied with two titans of the cello world — Mstislav Rostropovich and Gregor Piatigorsky — Maisky earned a reputation as an outspoken cellist, which conferred on him the status of an illustrious renegade.

In the question-and-answer period following the formal playing of the students, I was pleased to hear Maisky acknowledge the challenges of age. He emphatically noted that the older one got, the harder it was to learn a new piece, *especially by memory*. Jokingly — or was he serious? — he advised the young men and women in attendance: "If you want to learn a piece by memory, do it before you're fifty or forty or even thirty!"

For the moment, I felt less of a musical misfit with my memory struggles.

Dobrochna backed off for a while. However, scales were *de rigueur* committed to memory, as were certain exercises.

Eventually, my arms and hands, muscles and tendons,

absorbed and committed to memory the accumulation of learning tips by persistent repetition and practice. My bow stayed on the strings longer without sliding south; the weighting of my bowing arm increased in its triangular configuration of wrist, elbow, and shoulder; my fingers dropped deeper onto the fingerboard. And yet, for every one improvement in sound and technique, dozens more waited to be overcome.

As I listened to more recordings, I inevitably matched my simple and simplistic way of playing with that of these masters who provided me with much inspiration. Immeasurable hours of continuous bowing variations, dynamic variants, and the addition of another clef — not just the bass but also the *tenor* clef dynamic variants — all awaited me over the following weeks. And yet, these turned out to be the least of my challenges.

5

Stresses and Strains

"*P*icture yourself playing the cello, Mavis," Dobrochna reminded me once more. "Yes, I want you to visualize yourself playing this instrument, as if you and it were one. Sit in front of a mirror and see yourself playing the cello, both in your body and in your mind's eye."

Picture Yourself Playing the Cello is the actual name of a primer book on cello learning with the subtitle *Step-by-Step Instruction for Playing the Cello*. It's a hands-on, practical guide to everything necessary to know about playing the cello, complete with diagrams, pictures, advice on bowings, positions, cello parts, and simple pieces of music.

I could certainly picture myself doing an awful lot of things: trampoline jumping, skydiving, rock climbing, all of which I'd attempted. I could see myself blowing into the tunnel of a flute, my fingers pressing down on the silver keys. I could imagine dancing a duet à la Mark Morris dancers. I could even visualize climbing Mount Kilimanjaro, the dormant volcanic peak in Tanzania, or kayaking off the shores of Vancouver Island.

But could I picture myself playing the cello? Could I imagine wrapping my body around a wooden instrument whose shape didn't exactly fit easily with mine without some serious manoeuvring?

I'd always been comfortable in my body, attached to the ease with which I could climb in and step out of a canoe or a kayak. I loved sensations of movement and conversely resented any restrictions on my mobility. I enjoyed the freedom of hiking, low or high altitude, having transported my body to the summit of Annapurna Base Camp in the Himalayas, having traversed the Burstall and Kananaskis Passes in the Canadian Rockies and the Walter Benjamin Trail from France into Spain. I'd hiked the granite towers, icebergs, and grey glaciers of Torres del Paine National Park in Patagonia as well as the corrugated trails of the Tatra Mountains, crossing the Polish-Slovakian border. To quote an overused phrase, I'd always loved "the wind at my back and the sun or rain on my face."

To date, I could always depend on the reliability of my body to navigate and enjoy the more demanding and phys- ically challenging activities on offer. While not immune to the normal colds and flus, drifting aches and pains, my body hadn't betrayed me yet in all the ways I knew it could and would much sooner than expected.

Spinal fusion surgery for scoliosis — more commonly known as curvature of the spine — at sixteen was the only major exception to a clean health record. Two permanent stainless-steel rods supporting either side of my spinal cord resided permanently within my body. The benefit of a year's entrapment in a body cast was good posture, the downside a life deprived of backbends or somersaults, yoga cat or cobra poses, horseback riding and bungee jumping.

I was a student of ballet and then contemporary dance in my teens and into my early thirties, a gym enthusiast throughout the remainder of my thirties and forties, and a committed Pilates enthusiast from my fifties onward. Despite that, I discovered cello playing to be exceedingly laborious, demanding new physical accents and strains. My body not only reacted but rebelled loudly, tempestuously, and defiantly, letting me know it couldn't be easily won over by this new activity or assuaged by what I perceived as the enjoyable benefits of my new relationship.

My knee hit one side of the instrument as I leaned more

to one cheek of my buttocks, and my legs refused to stay comfortable planted several metres apart on the floor for extended periods. Fortunately, the spinal fusion surgery provided certain advantages. For long stretches, I could easily sit with a straight spine near the edge of the chair without collapsing or slouching. On the other hand, my ability to mould my upper body to a more forward position was often compromised.

Over time, the body adjusts. Whether with long fingers and short arms, angular knees and long legs, restricted inner ligaments and tendons, long or short torsos, cellists come in all shapes and sizes. In other words, all cello playing results in physical negotiation if not outright battle.

As recommended by Dobrochna, my first few months of practice routine was limited to a thirty- to forty-minute schedule. After my first summer break, I began increasing my time to longer and longer stretches of practice.

Unknown to me, a perfect storm was developing in my body. It began with the tips of my fingers: a novel sensation, a tingling, an unusual burning reminiscent of the first time I accidentally handled an unripe Israeli cactus fruit, or prickly pear. A group of us were hiking in the Negev Desert, and I was admiring the varietals of tall cacti with their unusual shapes standing sentinel-like in the hot sunlight.

I noticed one almost-ripe fruit hanging off a particular bush several metres away. Deliciously inviting, I ran over and decided to bring it back to the group as a tasty treat. Gently, I plucked the tempting fruit and jogged back to the group, gift in outstretched hand. Everyone began laughing. I wondered why no one else had thought of this. *And zing!* My palm was covered in invisible prickles that made my hand feel as if it were on fire. Within minutes, my hand was burning up, especially the fingertips that had grasped the fruit first.

"You know you're going to really suffer for a few hours," one of the Israelis said, laughing. Little did I know that cacti had an invisible layer of prickles for self-protection.

That was the same sensation now erupting in the finger-tips of my right hand.

According to most manuals of instruction, bow holding, the primary "item of interest" in cello technique, is described as the simple and natural placement of the fingers: "Just drop your fingers like the paw of a dog and then pretend you're holding an orange."

Yet the little frog, the widening angle part of the bow pearlized with abalone, was a clear and obvious obstacle to the thumb and pressure on the bow, demanding pressure without tension. Finger burning became an antic-ipated barometer of my incorrect and squeezing bow hold, increasing with tension and concentration.

This complaint was to become the first, albeit a minor one in a litany of protests from my body. The uproar on the right side of my frame was the second major hurdle with which I had to contend. My upper and lower arm, my shoulder, and the right side of my torso were also engaged in a fierce battle.

I felt as if my body and I had come to represent two enemy teams in combat. Rather than working harmoniously, we were engaged in a skirmish to which neither side could concede. Unused, unknown, unnamed muscles ligaments and tendons were making themselves known, introducing themselves in direct and savage ways.

Maybe I wasn't abiding by Dobrochna's decree of picturing myself playing cello. Or maybe the image was inside out or upside down. Whatever it was, I knew I needed some assistance.

"Margot, I have to see you urgently," I wrote to my Pilates instructor from whom I'd taken years of classes. On the rare occasion that some muscle or tendon was strained or shouting at me, a session with Margot always resolved the issue as long as I followed the exercises she assigned. She appreciated the unique anatomy of my body with its metal rods in my back and the shoulder misalignment following a ski accident as a preteen.

MAVIS HIMES

"No problem," she said, "and please bring your cello to the studio so I can have a good look at how you're moving while playing."

Daisy accompanied me to my session. "Yes, I can see you're moving your right arm with certain restrictions." She sighed as she moved my arm in a series of rotations, asking me to imitate her movements and trying to identify the culprits interfering with comfortable motion.

At the end of our time, Margot described the underlying issues and reassured me that if I consistently followed the exercises we'd started, I'd return to a pain-free state. The next day, a list of exercises arrived in my email inbox. First, a cautionary set of provisos about the number of repetitions: a bit of fatigue was good, strain was terrible, and any nerve sensations were a marker to stop what I was doing immediately. Following that were a list of exercises with details: rub my eight wrist bones, circle my arm sideways while leaning, move my shoulder blades is if they were bars of soap, outward spirals with my forearms, and conduct an orchestra with my wrists.

Dobrochna was sympathetic. She added some new warm-up exercises to my practice routine. "Your over-eagerness to practise has placed unrealistic demands on your body," she said, as if chastising me for my enthusiasm. "When you study cello as a child, your muscles expand with normal muscle growth. You, on the other hand, are training for a marathon without giving your body a break."

Once again, I felt penalized for my late start. Was this a stupid idea in the first place? Maybe I should never have embarked on this journey. Then I remembered my friend, Ann, telling me how the cello was a much more natural position than the violin, which involved considerable strain on the neck and shoulders. At least I hadn't taken up the violin!

6

Piano Lessons

My musical beginnings coincided with early forays into the world of classical dance. I was still in kindergarten and learning the alphabet and number counting when my mother enrolled me in ballet lessons, joining Susan Ritz, my best friend. Trudging across an expanse of open fields on Saturday mornings, the two of us arrived at Miss Barbara Fletcher's house in the nearby neighbourhood of Snowdon in Montreal where, along with six other girls, we were welcomed inside.

Clothed in pink leotards, black bodysuits, and pink ballet slippers, we stood beside the barre and practised the seven positions of the feet and legs, the five stations of the arms, and the five expressions of the heart. It was in this context that I learned the rudiments of that most ardent and amorous of languages as our teacher shouted out the commands: *Pliez, étirez, soulevez, glissez.*

After an initial warm-up at the barre, the eight of us congregated in the middle of the room and freely moved our bodies to the recorded sounds of ballet music. And it was there in the safety of Miss Barbara's panelled basement, liberated from the everyday world of parental voices and the strict rules of dance, that we twirled and leaped, swayed and pirouetted, imagining ourselves on a stage watched by hundreds. And it was there that I was also introduced to the music of Léo Delibes and Pyotr Ilyich Tchaikovsky, Georges

Bizet and Frédéric Chopin, whose melodic tunes held power over my twirling body.

At home on my portable LP record player, I listened repeatedly to the popular ballets of *Giselle* and *Coppélia*, the *Nutcracker* and *Swan Lake*. Like Cinderella, I closed my eyes and saw visions of a handsome Prince Charming lifting me off the floor and tossing me into the air as I'd seen in films. Then we floated gracefully across the floor in a magnificently performed pas de deux.

My dreams of becoming a prima ballerina came to an abrupt end with the diagnosis of scoliosis toward the end of high school. Annual checkups and exercises ensued, culminating in a year of a body brace followed by the ultimate corporal intrusion of surgery: spinal fusion, bone grafting, and another year of armour in an ambulatory body cast.

While still in grade school and prior to the fiasco with my back, piano lessons were added to my repertoire of after-school activities — my formal debut as a student of music.

Mrs. Petrovsky arrived punctually at 4:00 p.m. every Tuesday. A Russian émigré, divorced and living with her developmentally challenged son, she travelled "three bus transfers across town," as my mother repeated regularly, to arrive at our house for my lessons. I once overheard my mother tell my father that her husband had slapped her around and then returned to his native Estonia — perhaps to a lover, I speculated — while she continued to work at two part-time jobs in addition to piano teaching to support herself and her son.

The imposing stature of Mrs. Petrovsky was augmented by her height. Hair always perfectly coiffed in a chignon with a large tortoiseshell hair ornament keeping it all in place, she spoke in clipped phrases as if in time to the metronome she placed on the piano for each lesson. Each week I observed her beside me in her silk shirts, transparent and cream-coloured, with a lacy bodice underneath guarding against any improper carnal exposure. Skirts, cinched at the waist with a tight belt, revealed her mature figure. During lessons, her rather ample chest, rising and falling as she beat her finger on the music stand, arrested my attention as she encouraged me. I tried to imagine the heartache she might have suffered as I plonked away at the piano keys.

"Faster, faster," she might say loudly, her camisole bobbing up and down in rhythm with her heaving bosom.

Mrs. Petrovsky taught me the trio of musical commandments: dedication, discipline, and diligence. She explained that music could never be mastered but could always improved. And in her accented voice, she clarified that self-control, self-restraint, and a regimen of regular piano practice could one day turn me into a talented pianist.

MAVIS HIMES

In the winter of my thirteenth year, I underwent my annual piano examination at the Royal Conservatory of Music in Montreal. Each year, Mrs. Petrovsky anxiously anticipated this event, priming me with technical studies and increased homework, as if my performance results were a measure of her own talents as a teacher. Although I'd already completed several levels of the conservatory with stellar grades, Mrs. Petrovsky continued to tirelessly ring her hands as the date approached.

The night before the scheduled examination, my mother cut my nails and laid out my outfit for the following day. As if she was in a conspiratorial pact with my teacher, I found a white chiffon blouse placed on the chair with a navy skirt and thick belt.

"I passed my exam with exemplary grades," I broadcasted when I returned home. And there was Mrs. Petrovsky beaming like a silly old fool, so I thought, and waiting expectantly with my mother in our kitchen.

"Practice makes perfect," she reminded me in her crisply accented speech. "This is your reward. And now we must continue to practise while we work on our next level. Yes, practise, practise."

I stared at the straps of her camisole as they slid off her shoulders under her starched shirt, deciding then and there to no longer tolerate her insistent commands. In fact, I was determined to go on strike and refuse to play my piano routines. Then, a couple of months later, I threatened to quit altogether if I couldn't change piano teachers. I balked at being held captive by Mrs. Petrovsky's constant demands.

When my mother informed Mrs. Petrovsky that I wished to discontinue lessons, she cried. "I think it might be a good learning experience for Mavis to have exposure to a different frame of reference. A new teacher might give her another perspective and instill some renewed vitality," my mother explained, trying to soften the blow.

"That's all I want for your daughter," I overheard Mrs.

Petrovsky say between sniffles. "She's so talented. The most important thing is that she continues her musical studies. I had such plans for her." And she blew her nose vigorously into her white handkerchief.

Changing teachers was a positive decision in more ways than one. If Mrs. Petrovsky reminded me of a character from a tragedy by Anton Chekhov, Mrs. Czerniak, another Russian émigré, was an incarnation of Mimi, the Bohemian seamstress in La Bohème. Mrs. Czerniak had immigrated to Canada via Hungary and was as different from Mrs. Petrovsky as Sergei Rachmaninoff was from Johann Sebastian Bach.

In contrast to my lessons with Mrs. Petrovsky that occurred at my house, I had to travel to Mrs. Czerniak's home. This involved two bus transfers and a twenty-minute walk through the treed streets of Outremont. Carrying my school books and sheet music in a tote bag, I now saw myself as part of the adult world of bus travellers.

On my first visit, I double-checked the house number as I approached the steps of her home, glancing under the porch to confirm number seventy-eight. Standing breathlessly, I waited for someone to answer the door.

A strikingly beautiful woman with Romani looks answered and immediately introduced herself. "You must be Mavis. Please come in," she said in a crystal-clear voice with an accent I couldn't identify yet. "I'm Mrs. Czerniak, but you can call me Ana."

She led me into a spartan room with hardwood floors, high ceilings, and terracotta painted walls. The room was bare except for the two shiny grand pianos facing each other on a diagonal, as if to enhance the opportunity of a dialogue.

Too self-conscious to address an adult by her first name, I continued to call my new acquaintance Mrs. Czerniak, the name I still remember to this day.

Ana Czerniak exuded an energy that twirled around her petite frame. Jet-black hair, long and wavy, caressed the middle of her back, her tortoiseshell glasses resting low on her aquiline nose. She wore black fishnet stockings with pointed shoes and flowing skirts that swished around her legs as she moved. The first time we met, I noted the clingy black sweater hugging her narrow frame because it matched the fabric of my black dance leotards. Around her shoulders draped a magnificent emerald-green shawl. As she walked over to greet me, I felt as if I were observing an exotic peacock strutting before me in full view. Her lips, full and diamond-shaped, were painted a ruby red that matched her neatly manicured nails, and when she smiled, her lips parted ever so slightly to reveal small teeth.

At our initial lesson, Mrs. Czerniak invited me to sit at one of the pianos while she settled at the other. "Play something. Play anything you like."

I was confused by the request. *No scales? No arpeggios? How could I play without first warming up my fingers?*

"I'd like to hear how you approach the music," she said, putting forth a simple request in a calm voice. And in the simplicity of that invitation, I felt mature and adult-like. Simultaneously, in the openness of this freedom, I was completely unsettled.

Sensing my dilemma, she pulled a book from the stack I'd brought with me. "Here, what can you play from this?"

I selected a Domenico Scarlatti sonatina. Nervously, I tried to mark the rhythm in my head, tapping the keys with my fingers. Finally, I placed my fingers on the keys and floundered through the piece with several errors, blushing as I glanced up.

"Bravo! she exclaimed when I finished. "Well done, indeed!"

Again, she invited me to play another piece to which she once more complimented me despite further blatant errors.

As we began the formal teaching, she moved over to my bench and sat beside me. Speaking in a soft voice, almost as if whispering, she demonstrated some finger movements for me to imitate, almost as if initiating me into the hand gestures of a secret society.

And so began a new and complex relationship of student and teacher.

When I arrived for my weekly lessons, Mrs. Czerniak always assumed I'd practised my exercises, so she only asked me to repeat scales and arpeggios as finger and hand warm-ups. Instead of the repetitive études that focused on techniques, she introduced me to the music of such Russian titans as Sergei Rachmaninoff and Nikolai Rimsky-Korsakov with their oversized hand stretches, the Hungarian and Polish romanticists, and Viennese classicists such as Wolfgang Amadeus Mozart and Ludwig van Beethoven with whom I was already familiar.

She often demonstrated a new piece by playing on the second piano. I listened in awe and suspense to the intoxicating sounds brought forth by her hands, hypnotized by the sensual mood created by the music, an ambience matched by the warmth of the ceiling-to-floor rich burgundy velvet drapes that blocked out the sunlight and the mundane elements of the outside world.

Whenever I approached her house at the end of the dead-end street, I had the feeling I was about to enter a foreign world, a universe of exotic unfamiliarity. Here was a woman who wasn't afraid to show her feminine shapeliness or to accentuate the fullness of her lips. On more than one occasion, I noticed an ashtray with the butt of a used cigarette glistening with red lipstick suspended by a holder.

One day, as I stood waiting at the front door, I heard a voice shouting, a male tenor flinging out angry invectives, followed by a violent slamming of doors. Within minutes, Mrs. Czerniak welcomed me into her home. "So nice to see you again. How are you, darling?"

I never told my mother about the altercation I overheard. I coveted this as a secret treasure and cherished the feeling of having access to a world to which I didn't yet belong, a place of furtiveness and intrigue.

In my adolescent mind, I fantasized that Mrs. Czerniak lived in a world swarming with lovers. I imagined she was once an orphaned aristocrat surrounded by servants and travelling around the countryside in a carriage with a handsome Dr. Zhivago, and that she had a collection of Russian amber hidden in a samovar in the basement of her house.

This was another Russia, far from the strictures and limitations imposed by Mrs. Petrovsky's rigidity and emotional sterility. It was the Russia of Alexander Borodin and Igor Stravinsky, Boris Pasternak and Leo Tolstoy. This was the wrenching passion of suffering and love, of counts and countesses, dukes and duchesses, the largesse of a pre-revolutionary empire.

My lessons continued unabated for two years at which point my mother put her foot down and decided my lessons were to be discontinued. She claimed I wasn't practising enough *at all* and that my mind seemed to drift elsewhere. And while I treasured my time with this eccentric pianist, I couldn't disagree about my diminishing interest in the keyboard with all its rhapsodic melodies and contrapuntal rhythms I'd been exploring. And, consequently, my musical career came to an abrupt halt.

Mrs. Czerniak, wrapped in a black embroidered shawl as if in mourning, her eyes moist and dewy, embraced me passionately. "I know you'll do well. You have the right temperament, an artistic sensitivity rare in women of your age."

I kissed her cheek and rushed out.

Woman. No one had ever referred to me as such. I walked with a lightness, smiling and dancing down the sidewalk. I knew Ana Czerniak was able to discern something about me that my mother couldn't see. Only Ana could detect a hidden talent that neither of my parents recognized yet.

Throughout this same period of high school, I'd also been listening unabatedly to the classical music of Johann Sebastian Bach, Joseph Haydn, Antonín Dvořák, Franz Schubert, Frédéric Chopin, and others while my friends rocked and rolled to The Byrds, The Supremes, and The Monkees. When left alone in the house, I stretched out on the living room sofa and put on the LPs of my favourite music composers. My parents gave me money to establish their record collection, entrusting me with the title of "music director."

One night during this self-imposed music-training program — piano lessons, practice, and record listening — I attended my first live concert. An unexpected series of events resulted in an extra ticket to a live performance featuring Vladimir Ashkenazy, the celebrated Russian pianist and musical idol of Mrs. Petrovsky, with Rhoda, my mother's close friend. The following night at our house, my mother insisted on a *fancy* outfit for my debut attendance at Place des Arts, Montreal's main music venue at the time.

The details of that night remain blurry in my memory except for a few things: the evening was cold, I wore a winter coat and high boots, Rhoda parked the car quite far away, and we had to walk through snow-covered streets. When the light was about to change, we ran across an intersection and made it just as the lights in the lobby flickered. A man of medium stature appeared onstage, bowed, and sat with no introduction, then immediately began to play. From our seats, I couldn't see his hands but heard his fingers cascade back and forth across the keys, head bobbing as in prayer.

More than the music, what I remember was what occurred after the concert. Rhoda grabbed my arm as we descended five or six steps below ground level into a bohemian hangout on Crescent Street where we were welcomed into a dimly lit room.

Rhoda and I talked while waiters in black-waisted aprons, white shirts, and black vests rushed around with trays of steaming coffee mugs and fancy pastries. After a few minutes, a waiter approached and leaned into the table, requesting our order. Rhoda suggested I try a cappuccino with a slice of apple strudel. "And maybe one scoop of ice cream on the side?" she added, smiling up at the man with bushy hair and eyebrows.

The apple strudel when it came was stuffed high with cinnamon-flavoured fruit and encased in pastry that bore no resemblance to my grandmother's version. Roma music by live musicians played in the background, and red-and-white-checked tablecloths with wine bottles wrapped in rattan and stuffed with dripping white candles sat on all the tables.

Surrounded by an aura of pseudo-maturity, I thrust myself into an imaginary future, casting myself into the role of an artist holding court with my friends of similar ilk, sipping wine and discussing Rimsky-Korsakov's *Scheherazade*.

Halfway through our soirée, Rhoda turned to me with a serious expression, a cigarette dangling from her fingers. She was my mother's only friend who smoked, and I envied the elegance with which she opened her silver cigarette case and pulled out a slender stick as our *garçon* hurried over with a lighter. "How did you enjoy the concert … really?" she asked me. "Did you enjoy it? What did you like best?"

Choosing words that echoed what Rhoda had already mentioned, I innocently tried to convey my great appreciation and pleasure. As she reiterated comments about the music, I vigorously nodded, listening to her remarks carefully, associating her words with features of the natural world — fields and rivers, storms and streams. Enchanted by her descriptions, I vowed to learn more about the musical repertoire so that I, too, could articulate the magic and mystery of what we'd just heard.

Alas, by the end of high school, I shrugged off the austerity and heaviness of Mozart and Haydn, Bach and Beethoven, and threw myself headlong into a new universe with newly discovered heroes. In my pitch-black basement room with cedar-strip panels, low ceilings, and Piet Mondrian cupboards, I lay on a sofa imbibing the mellow, grainy voice of Leonard Cohen sing his heart out to Suzanne, Marianne, and other girlfriends. I studied the revolutionary lyrics of Bob Dylan whose songs infected and inflected a generation of youth with phrases chronicling societal faults and fissures. In my basement retreat, I shut out the voice of my mother begging me to do chores and that of my teacher inviting me to complete another assignment. Whether piano, ballet, or Hebrew lessons, I dismissed all the commands and directives, hearing only the words of Cohen's "Hey, That's No Way to Say Goodbye."

University life followed shortly. Assailed by global sociopolitical events of revolutionary proportions, music soon became entwined with various social movements: human, women's, and civil rights. Songs of protest endorsed and accompanied these seismic shifts, announcing a new era.

Throughout these early college years, discussions with friends revolved around the Vietnam War and conscientious objectors, the Americans freely traversing our borders, the philosophies of Jean-Paul Sartre and Simone de Beauvoir, while the voices of Janis Joplin, Rod Stewart, Mick Jagger, and Eric Clapton filled the airwaves and blasted out on transistor radios. Music permeated my nights with tunes of hope and peace, protest and revolution.

And then a second seismic shift occurred. I fell in love madly, deeply, insanely. Along with an expanded repertoire of amorous adventures and shared escapades, a musical chapter opened up, characterized by the same rawness and sensuality of this new relationship.

It began with a chance encounter one morning. Meeting

my friend, Lisette, in the Student Union cafeteria of McGill University, we were joined by her boyfriend and his friend.

"Hi, I'm DB," he said, offering his hand in a formal introduction.

And I stared at this handsome man in his Leonidas boots, loden green, oversized army coat and plaid scarf with unkempt hair and fashionable beard. I couldn't resist his charm and intellect. We quickly became enchanted with each other, and it was through this relationship that I walked away from the world of the Classics, Romantics, Modernists, and Serialists and entered a musical realm of folk, rock, soft metal, heavy metal, and whatever else provided the background for the days and nights we spent together.

Streets away from the university annex, we trudged and tramped our way to his studio apartment on rue de Bullion. Studying, chatting, eating, and sleeping, we cocooned in the crowded space that also became the hub of our musical library. Striding over to his collection, DB inevitably decided on the mood by choosing an album from the makeshift record display fashioned by planks of wood bookended by bricks along the baseboard of one wall.

Novel sound vibrations permeated my body, inviting me to move and shake, rattle and roll. Gone was the tameness of my piano-playing days, replaced by the dynamics of unlimited vibrations.

Like a connoisseur of fine libations, he introduced me into the ways of savouring and enjoying the rhythms, sounds, and lyrics of each musician. So, sprawled across a double bed draped with a green-and-tangerine comforter and scattered Persian pillows, I listened to folk duo Jim and Jean, The Moody Blues, Creedence Clearwater, Van Morrison, and so many others.

"How about this?" he'd ask for the sake of form without any anticipation of disagreement from me.

"Sounds great," I inevitably chirped in deference to his mastery of the sound system and output.

On our first Valentine's Day evening, DB placed an LP on the record player. "Listen to this one. I picked it especially for this occasion," he said, moving his arm around my waist and pulling me over to the bed. An empty bottle lay tossed on the floor, while dirty dishes were piled off to the side and candle wax dripped onto the makeshift wooden end table. We turned off the lights in the candlelit room, and with eyes closed at DB's instructions, I remained immobile on the bed, waiting for the music to begin. It was Bob Dylan's "Lay, Lady, Lay" as sung by Johnny Cash, whose voice suffused the room as our bodies gyrated, lifting us out of our daily rhythms. So it was that DB's collection of LPs and tapes, the envy of his friends, became the background in which our relationship ran its course.

Within two years, music and men took a back seat as I gave myself over to my education and commitment to a professional career. While academic work became my dominant focus over the next decade, music remained a constant diversion to which I always returned for pleasure, one I eventually came back to. Shortly after completing my undergraduate degree, I moved to Toronto to pursue graduate studies in psychology.

7

Jacqueline du Pré

*D*ressed up for the occasion in leggings and black tunic
with shoulder cut-outs and a multicoloured shawl, I met
Dobrochna at the entrance of Toronto's Betty Oliphant
Theatre. Arriving half an hour in advance of the performance,
we each ordered a glass of Bordeaux and sipped our wine
while watching the men and women with rainbow-streaked
hair, tight-fitting pants, and cashmere scarves mingle.

Dobrochna and I were attending the world premiere
of *Jacqueline*, a Tapestry Opera production showcasing the
extraordinary talent and decline of Jacqueline du Pré, the
renowned British cellist . Hers was a well-documented story
among musical *aficionados*: a child prodigy revered by all; a
formal debut in the most prestigious concert halls of London,
England, at sixteen; a stellar performance of Edward Elgar's
Cello Concerto at the Royal Festival Hall at seventeen, cata-
pulting her into immediate international acclaim; and a
whirlwind career with a coterie of eminent musicians. And
then the unfortunate appearance of tingling numbness in
her fingers beginning at the age of twenty-three and culminating in a diagnosis of multiple sclerosis four years later. A
remarkable woman whose career was forcibly and tragically
cut short at the age of forty-two in 1987, she was mourned
and honoured throughout the music world.

I was curious to watch this production of Jackie's life,
since I'd already read the biography of her by Elizabeth
Wilson; seen the film *Remembering Jacqueline du Pré* by

Christopher Nupen; and watched the controversial movie *Hilary and Jackie*, depicting her musical essence and impassioned and fervent life. I had also just witnessed the intense love affair between Jackie and her cello in a live-streamed production of *The Cellist* performed by Britain's Royal Ballet during Covid-19.

Tapestry's *Jackie* followed the concerto structure of four movements, as in the Elgar Concerto: her childhood, the shadow of disease hovering over her meteoric success, her retreat from the public, and her incapacitating illness. I was spellbound by the production. The American actor-singer Marnie Breckenridge's radiant beauty and joy, transcending age and character, exploded with energy and personality in her portrayal of Jackie, while the Canadian Matt Haimovitz, another living child prodigy who himself had studied briefly with du Pré, represented Jackie's voiced and constant companion, her cello. In fact, Jackie owned four different cellos in her professional lifetime, the love never fading fully with any of them. The intensity and lyricism of Matt's musical portrayal of Jackie's physical and mental journey permeated my being long after the curtain fell.

Jackie profoundly penetrated the mystery of the cello. The alchemy between her and her instrument surpassed a simple summary of her playing. Whether swooning and ecstatic or vulnerable and caressing, an intimate and all-engrossing understanding cemented the connection existing between this young woman and her instrument. This blissful relationship, in fact, surpassed the ostensible love affair with her husband, the Argentine-born conductor and pianist Daniel Barenboim. It was the cello that became her closest friend, partner of her greatest successes, witness and ally in her losses, and in the end, the symbol of her ongoing legacy.

By the end the show, I was a sponge of heightened emotion. To be deprived of one's beloved, to be parted from one's soulmate, and to then be reduced to an object of compassion at such a young age could only be viewed as an unmerited tragedy. How was I to know I'd experience a nano-fraction of that unforeseen separation myself?

After the performance, Dobrochna suggested we hang around the lobby to meet the musicians. She had almost studied with Matt at McGill University in Montreal but had opted instead to come to Toronto under the tutelage of Shauna Rolston. In her free-wheeling spirit, Dobrochna waited for the small cast to appear and pronto approached Matt, while I hid behind her tall frame.

"Hello, my name's Dobrochna Zubek," I heard her say. "I very much enjoyed your performance. We met, you and I ..." I no longer remember the words, the rest of the conversation, but I do recall the photo she requested of the three of us, a memento of the evening, a token of our outing to hear a rendition of du Pré's brilliant musicianship.

On the way home, it occurred to me that I had the same initials as Matt Haimovitz: MH. And then I realized the similarity of our surnames. Heimovitch was our original family name before my father and his eight siblings shortened it to Himes to safeguard us from the anti-Semitic sentiment prevalent in postwar Montreal.

Maybe we're related? I thought. *Is it possible that some genetic in-mixing may have spread to my biochemical stew, allowing me to inherit some of Matt's ferocious talent?*

That second summer of 2019, over a year into my cello studies and before the Covid pandemic globally transformed the lives of men and women, children and animals, I took advantage of the summer music festivals that thrived annually in the city and surrounding areas.

Dobrochna had informed me of a concert she was performing with some colleagues from Thin Edge New

Music Collective. While certainly composed of contemporary music, she told me it wasn't inaccessible.

Two weeks later, on a steamy summer evening in June, my friend Jacquie and I entered the air-conditioned lobby of The Theatre Centre and then the darkened performance area to hear *Triptych* performed by a small group of musicians — piano, violin, flute, violin, cello, and percussion — to which electroacoustics were subsequently added. I'd relayed Dobrochna's caveat to Jacquie, who wasn't a fan of new music.

A cacophony of sound, atonal and provocative, experimental and unorthodox, bounced off the walls in the blackened space.

Jacquie left at intermission. I stayed for the rest of the concert to see a multi-disciplinary performance in which "tactile transducers, live processing, and self-built mechanics" were incorporated into a piece that was as much about the body feel of sound spaces as about audible sound. A final piece integrated digital systems with audiovisual performances giving the players a chance to interact experimentally with the work of the composer.

I didn't leave. However, my endurance for the pieces entitled *Thruline* and *New Notations* was tested.

When I next spoke to Dobrochna, I lambasted her for not giving me a more apt description of the program.

"After all, Mavis, think of the group's name — Thin Edge New Music Collective," she retorted. "What did you expect?"

A week or two later, I attended my first public master class with the Chamber Music Institute Fellows. Bryan Lee, first violinist of the Dover Quartet, took the stage and made some introductory remarks. I quietly entered the auditorium and sat in the second row with a quick glance at the program:

Claude Debussy's String Quartet in G Minor, Mozart's String Quintet in D Major, and Dvořák's Piano Quartet No. 2 in E-Flat Major. The young musicians calling themselves the Iceberg String Quartet then appeared. I smiled as I pulled my sweater tighter around me in the chilly air-conditioned room.

Holding my breath, I listened as the group played the first piece: rising crescendos and falling pianissimos. After some positive comments, a Talmudic exposition and a phrase-by-phrase dissection of the performance followed. Turning to the numbered bars, Bryan Lee addressed the students with a supportive but directive tone. I was positive the young musicians feigned composure and self-containment as their playing was magnified under a microscope.

Along the tree-lined path of Philosopher's Walk after the class, I randomly expressed my thoughts to a student I'd seen sitting close by. "Wow, I can't imagine being under such scrutiny. It must be so nerve-wrenching to play under the probing analysis of a master."

Anxiously pulling at his T-shirt, he chimed back, "Oh, we students are used to that. Just sweaty palms and elevated heart rate for a few moments and then it's over."

My musical summer interlude continued a few days later as I marched over to Heliconian Hall in Yorkville to listen to high-energy vibes and an eclectic program performed by the Ladom Ensemble. A hip young group of musicians — piano, cello, accordion, and percussion — entertained the crowded room with a uniquely original blend of acoustic chamber and world music. There were hints of Argentine tango spiced with Serbian folk and dance traditions, Persian classical repertoire, and a dash of classical Johann Sebastian Bach and Sergei Prokofiev, with some notes from the rock world of Radiohead. It was a mash-up of buzzing and catchy sounds that left me bouncing and humming all evening.

During the concert, I observed the movements of the cellist Beth Silver who "rocked" with her instrument. Boldly dressed in a crimson satin skirt and sporting big hair, Beth drew me to her playing even in the midst of the artistry of all the other musicians. Something about her playing style reminded me of Dobrochna. My hunch was confirmed when Dobrochna verified that, despite being several years her junior, Beth had also studied with Shauna Rolston.

There was hope for me yet.

8

First House Concert

*A*fter eighteen months, I hit a brick wall. I was in complete revolt. I didn't want to touch or have anything to do with my instrument. I was fed up and no longer interested.

I questioned the whole enterprise. *What was I thinking? How did I ever think I'd be able to master playing the cello at such a late date in my life?*

I was furious that I still couldn't master the third and fourth positions on the cello, that I couldn't nail G on the D string, that my bowing was inconsistent, and that there was always something new required of me. It didn't help that Dobrochna had been late for my last lesson, that it had taken ten minutes for her to tune my cello to hers via Skype, and that I couldn't perform three notes in succession correctly after weeks of practice.

"That's it. I'm done," I announced like a petulant child.

I crossed my fingers on the computer screen. Of course, the enforced change to virtual lessons due to the coronavirus pandemic didn't help my mood. The personal detachment and poor sound quality of the computer's audio function made lessons more impersonal and less satisfying, though better than none.

Nor did it help that my beloved husband, fifteen years my senior, was slowing down and could no longer keep up with my pace. Our shared activities were decreasing, and a deep sadness had settled within me. It was heartbreaking to see my soulmate aging and becoming weaker, making me more aware of time's passage and life's fragility. "And may you *sta-a-a-ay-y* forever young," crooned Joan Baez in my ear.

"Dear D.," I wrote after that particular lesson, "I don't want to practise, I don't want to play, I don't want to think about cello. I'm fed up and need a break. I'm done trying and struggling. I'm disappointed in myself. Maybe I'm just too old."

My rebellion only lasted a week. I quickly missed the intermission in my day when I could leave the business of my schedule and listen to my ongoing efforts to create music with my cello. I longed for the notes of Schumann and Bach and the sensation of resonance in my body when I played. And I felt ashamed for allowing my impatience and frustration to dominate and take control.

"Remember what you signed up for," Dobrochna announced the next time I saw her.

"Why don't we plan a house concert?" Dobrochna suggested a few weeks later. "Perhaps that'll be a first step toward your own hope to perform one day. What do you think?"

Always receptive to new projects and plans, I immediately said, "Great idea!" We agreed to give it some thought.

The seedling had been planted. Within a few weeks, Dobrochna found a duet partner, mapped out a themed program, and suggested a few dates convenient for both a violinist she knew, Adam Diderrich, and herself. Lawlor and I confirmed one of the dates.

Lo and behold, the first house concert at our home was about to transpire. I was thrilled to be following the predominantly German tradition of *Hausmusik*, a popular form of amateur music-making in the family home. In its original iteration, amateurs and professionals commingled in someone's home to share an afternoon or evening of fine quality music playing.

I'd already attended several house (pocket) concerts in Toronto where professional duets, trios, and quartets performed in elegant homes designed for such entertainment. In one, the home of an orchestral musician, I sat transfixed as the cello's plaintive sound interacted with the nobly restrained tone of a violin in a Schubert piano trio.

Lawlor and I both loved to host get-togethers and events. For the next several weeks, I busied myself with self-styled printed invitations, a refreshment menu, party rentals, and mailing lists. Finally, it all came together — the wine and cheese pairings, the platters of hors d'oeuvres, the assemblage of chairs in neat rows, the mini-floral arrangements.

"This isn't a food event, Mavis," my friend, Franceszka, reminded me. "No need to go overboard here. Did you forget that people are coming for the music?"

"This first concert is my treat," I told Dobrochna. "Honorariums for you and Adam, libations and food, rentals, the whole works on us. I really wish to do this and don't want to ask my friends for any contributions. The next time," I underscored, "if there's to be a next time, it'll be music and donations."

In the morning of a Sunday in August, I bustled madly around the house ensuring all was in order. Guests began arriving in festive summer wear, as if decked out for a recital hall concert. I watched from my bedroom window as Dobrochna and Adam jumped out of an Uber, visibly hot, and I scuttled them upstairs to our bedroom, the makeshift green room where musicians warmed up. As the musicians rehearsed, I engaged with my friends, desperately trying to conceal my nervousness.

With the dining room table thrust against one wall, the kitchen chairs hidden in the basement to make room for the stackable rentals, and a rudimentary stage area in the front of the living room, Lawlor and I had created the illusion of a performance space. A festive vibe filled the house. Freshly vacuumed seats on the stairs were on offer for any latecomers. By the time the musicians were ready to begin, thirty people had gathered.

At the insistence of Dobrochna, I had prepared an introductory presentation entitled *The Enchantment of Listening*. With a brass bell chime, I invited everyone to their seats, each chair topped with a printed program, a biography of the musicians on one side and the musical selection on the other.

ENCHANTING MUSIC FOR A SUNDAY AFTERNOON
Sunday, August 25, 2019

Cellist: Dobrochna Zubek
Violinist: Adam Diderrich

Introduction: *The Enchantment of Listening* (Mavis Himes)

Ludwig van Beethoven: Duet No. 2 for Violin and Cello
Allegro affetuoso
Aria larghetto
Rondo allegro moderato

Johann Sebastian Bach: Three Canons from *The Art of Fugue*
Canon in Hypodiapason — Canon alla Ottava
Canon alla duodecima in *Contrapunto alla Quinta*
Canon in Hypodiatessaron al roversio e per augmentationem, perpetuus

Ludwig van Beethoven: Duet No. 3 for Violin and Cello
Allegro sostenuto
Aria con varazioni

Heinrich Ignaz Franz Biber: Passacaglia from *Mystery Sonatas* **for Solo Violin**

Zoltán Kodály: Duo for Violin and Cello, Opus 7
Allegro serioso non troppo

Paper in hand, I welcomed everyone and improvised my talk in line with the theme of the concert. I mentioned the "three e's" that play a part in introducing new audiences to classical musical: education, exposure, and enthusiasm. While many friends patronized the concert halls of Toronto and were at home with the classical repertoire, I also knew that music listening could be demanding.

I was mindful of the reflections on music appreciation made by Stephen Hough in *Rough Ideas*:

> People understand that playing an instrument, like excelling in sport, requires years of work and dedication to reach a level of expertise. What they might not realise is that, unlike sport, when you can crack open your fifth beer, lie on the sofa and still enjoy the Wimbledon Finals, a Mahler symphony requires utter concentration to make its impact.[1]

Dobrochna had always insisted that listeners were part of the musical performance; they shaped the arc of its experience. To listen to a concert was to participate actively in the experience, not merely to be a passive bystander. While I tried to capture some of this in my talk, I worried whether I was inadvertently asking my friends to *play* a game of tennis rather than simply *watching* one. On the other hand, I wanted to provide an opportunity, like this, to make music accessible to more people.

After the intermission, Dobrochna introduced me as her student, and to the complete surprise of my friends and Lawlor, she and I played two short lyrical pieces from my *Piatti Étude for Two Cellos* book. Heart racing, hands shaking slightly, I gathered myself and my courage, like an artist about to showcase her most recent piece, and settled into my chair. Without quite enough of a preparatory gesture, I took the first up bow and began to play, the notes on the page a bit of a blur. I tried to slow my breathing but found it challenging with the adrenaline coursing through my body. Surrounded by friends, I knew my performance would be applauded no matter how I played, yet I still wanted to put forward my best effort. Despite some intonation errors, I was pleased I'd played through the piece without a halt, an accomplishment in its own right.

Lawlor threw me a kiss, and one or two friends gave me a thumbs-up. I stumbled back to my chair. Of course, everyone applauded my efforts.

A varied program followed with the aim of highlighting different types of dialogues that can occur between two instruments: from the folk-inspired duet by Kodály and the melodious passages of the Beethoven duets to the two-part harmonies of the Bach canons.

Everyone was enthralled by the shared experience of music listening. After the applause, no one spoke right away, as if wanting to relish the intimacy of the moment.

9

Body Pains

When we reunited after a summer break, Dobrochna suggested I remove the tape from my cello. While this had been discussed earlier, I wanted to wait until after the house concert. With ceremonial flourish, I slowly lifted the strips that had lined Daisy's neck for months.

This gesture ushered in a new period. I discovered a fresh sense of myself *playing cello*. Not only did I feel less like a beginner but I also experienced a deeper connection with my instrument for the first time. This translated into an intensification and depth of sound. Daisy and I were connecting on a more profound level.

Around the same time, Dobrochna recommended I keep a journal in which to record comments about my daily practice: what worked and what didn't, what questions emerged in the session, what I might have noticed, how my body felt. This was to be in addition to the lesson notebook I'd been keeping from the beginning.

I love bound notebooks — the feel, the texture, the design. With the same attention and care I gave to the notebooks of my professional seminars and workshops, I extravagantly sought out a special journal for my cello work.

Heading to Cubeshops, a boutique gallery store on Toronto's Baldwin Street specializing in housewares, office supplies, and tech accessories with a Japanese aesthetic, I selected a Rhodia, an iconic French journal competing with Moleskine, opting for one with a striped faux leather hardcover and unlined ivory vellum paper.

According to the saleswoman, this journal, like the store itself, was associated with creativity. "You're buying a journal that combines innovation with tradition," she remarked, carefully enfolding the journal in mauve tissue paper. She told me the Rhodia brand was very popular with artists and designers, emphasizing the superlative company with which I'd be keeping by my selection. I felt as if I were purchasing a passport of potential success. This journal would be the one for my lessons, I decided.

Subsequently, I googled Rhodia to satisfy my curiosity. I learned that this company, established in the early 1930s by the Verhilac brothers from Lyon, created its logo of two spruce trees linked by a line to represent the two brothers working side by side. I was thrilled as I pictured Dobrochna and me doing likewise.

In this journal, I recorded lesson notes as well as diary entries about the world of music in my daily life, pasting a small, typed sheet of paper in the front, a useful reminder of tips sent to me by Brenton:

Remember to slow down. Give yourself time to:

- Figure out where your fingers need to be (no jumping).
- Locate where you are in the music (should you get lost).
- And operating slower will allow you more opportunities to inhale and exhale (allowing your mind and body a small reprieve).

For my other journal, the recoding of my daily practice, I chose a notebook from my local bookstore: a gaily patterned one with a palette of lilac, sapphire, and turquoise that Dobrochna admired.

"Good choice," she concurred. "Light and lively. It'll inspire you, I'm sure."

In my mind, I chose a timeless design. I wanted it to

contain a vision of a future when I'd play with others in an amateur trio or quartet, entertaining my friends with tunes by Dvořák and Mozart. My diary notes for the first entry were:

August 22, 2019

Take time to prepare yourself. Take five minutes to warm up your body — arms, back, shoulders, wrists, hands — in order to prevent injuries. Create a space for yourself and slowly settle into your chair, position the cello and anchor yourself with your feet well planted on the floor. Try to minimize the stress and tension in your body as much as possible to avoid tightening up your muscles. Now play a scale and listen to your sound.

Dobrochna said the above like a mantra, repeating phrases she'd used months earlier. This time I absorbed a new level of concentration, intention, and deliberation required of my learning.

Perfectionism — a burning desire to play and master this instrument, to be able to perform multiple pieces. Driven to succeed, I knew I had to slow down and take the time required to strengthen my aging muscle groups. *How frustrating!*

I discovered a slowing down that came with permission and trust. Permission to take the time to let the world of recipes and shopping lists, patients and unfinished articles, settle, to allow the distractions of daily life fall like silt sinking to the ocean floor. I recognized the importance of breathing and the awakening of the body to a state of preparedness. However, I couldn't always maintain or sustain my desired intentions.

"My responsibility is to bring you to a place where you can play the best you can without injuries," Dobrochna told me. "I can help you develop, but I never know in advance how far that will be."

It was during the beginning of this second year that I began having problems with my left hand and wrist. In the late fall, I found myself in the waiting room of the Musicians' Clinic around the corner from my office. I received the clinic name from a woman I met at Concerts@100. At intermission, we spoke about injuries acquired by musicians as she rubbed her arm nestled in a sling. She described the physical difficulties she developed from her piano playing and volunteered the clinic name where, according to her, magic with musical injuries was performed.

After a delay of several months, I obtained an appointment with Dr. John McMillan, a former jazz alto saxophonist and pianist. With a mild sense of charade, I was thrilled at being seen by a specialist who worked exclusively with musicians. I felt I'd surreptitiously enrolled myself in a club for which I didn't quite have all the credentials or qualifications.

A man of slight proportions and generous smile welcomed me into a small room with a large piano pushed against a wall. After a thorough discussion of my practice habits and routines, my bodily complaints and existing remedial program, Dr. McMillan informed me my symptoms were common issues that could most likely be resolved with additional, or rather, different exercises.

I left his office with a note on a pink telephone message slip of paper. In legible handwriting were jotted down the following: upper-back strengthening with a notation about my rhomboids and middle "traps," a reminder to support and not grip my thumb at the neck of the cello, and the suggestion of the purchase of a blue exercise ball to work on releasing my pectorals and upper back.

Unfortunately, the magic received that day didn't work on my particular body.

Three months later, I visited Dr. Linda Dvali, a plastic surgeon specializing in hand issues. While manipulating my hand on her desk, she said in a monotone, "You have tendonitis of the thumb. The simplest intervention is to give you another cortisone injection. I can do that now if you like."

I'd seen Dr. Dvali once before when I had a condition popularly known as trigger finger, years prior to cello playing. That disorder, causing pain, stiffness, and a sensation of locking when bending and straightening a finger, was remedied by a cortisone shot. On this occasion, the inflammation in my wrist was clearly related to the muscles around the base of my thumb due to gripping and locking it around the neck of the cello. Looking at the doctor, I nodded in agreement, concerning the shot.

Applauding my new activity, Dr. Dvali encouraged my efforts on the cello. "You should be good to go after this," she said with a smile. "Just try to be careful."

I left with my hand protected in a wrist brace, trying to alleviate the built-up tension. Added to my treatment plan was a regular regimen of ibuprofen "as needed."

Later, Dobrochna continued to warn me. "Incorrect technique causes injuries. That's why we need to make sure your technique and positions are aligned."

"Always make sure you do proper warm-ups," another teacher wrote in a manual on the avoidance of injuries. I'd been doing warm-ups for months. Perhaps younger muscles responded to warm-ups, but older ones required a slow smoulder.

Dobrochna advised me to see a physiotherapist, as well.

At my next cello lesson, I arrived to find Dobrochna's arm adorned with kinesiology tape. She applied some to my wrist, and we were now musical twins. Dobrochna gave me another series of exercises to apply to the practice of my scales. "Don't forget to hang your fingers off the fingerboard," she repeated as she gave me a big hug upon leaving. "You must weight your fingers but not your thumb."

An impossible contradiction!

I returned to Margot for more exercises. She explained hands were like a complex symphony of delicate parts that worked together. "You know, with twenty-seven bones, twenty-nine joints, and at least one hundred and twenty-three named ligaments in the human hand, it gets pretty complicated when one part's out of kilter."

The body's response to repetitive strain, I believed, was an individual concoction of genetics, anatomy, posture, habit, and flexibility. Whatever the causes, injuries forced change as the body insisted on being heard and paid heed. As a result, I was forced to reconsider and re-evaluate. I felt as if I were back at the beginning, another downward spiral to basics: a return to scales, finger weighting, and back to the beginning but always with a difference. As I told my own patients, whatever reverted to its repetitive pattern provided us with another opportunity for change.

My speed, impatience, and self-indulgent desire for tangible progress had been forfeited for the sake of my physical health. Now I had to practise even slower. I had to inure and harden myself against further aches and pains. Like dancers with mangled toes and calloused feet, or athletes with strained ligaments and tendons, I discovered repetitive strain injuries to be nasty, persistent, and common in cellists of all ages and levels.

According to Joseph Johnson, currently the principal cellist of the Toronto Symphony Orchestra, poor habits breed troubled body parts later on down the road. Shoulders, arms, lower back, neck, hamstrings, all take a hit with repetitive movements in playing. Johnson told me that after years of travelling with his instrument, which entailed walking through airports, transferring weight in and out of taxis, buses, and subways, walking to and from concert halls, upstairs and downstairs, his back had eventually paid the penalty of it all.

For several months I was free of any discomfort on the right side of my body. The ache and soreness in my left wrist had also cleared up. I felt whole once again, ready to immerse myself in my practice.

"Now, when you move to the fourth position, it may feel awkward," Dobrochna told me one day. "You must retain the C shape in your left hand but at the same time, even with the interference of the cello's body, you must find a way of managing the two. Your knuckles aren't well developed enough to sit comfortably, but that will come in time."

Time. That word again!

My knuckles? Who thought they would require attunement? I wasn't a boxer, so why should my knuckles need calisthenic training? Yet every muscle group of the body appeared to be implicated and engaged. My whole body was being coerced, and not without significant pushback: once again, my fingers tingled and burned within minutes. Old pain resurfaced. The tips of my fingers still simply fell asleep, going numb in their resistance and refusal to co-operate. *Give us a rest. Let us sleep.*

At the same time, my thumb could still pulse where the pressure of the frog was most intense. Eventually, I had a rubber guard placed over the frog so the sharp edge didn't ride into my thumb.

When I went to pick up a neighbour's bow at Remenyi House of Music one day, I struck up a conversation with the woman behind the desk. It turned out she'd been a cello teacher for many decades.

"I'm really struggling with my bow hold," I confessed. "The position is still a challenge."

"Well, you might consider holding a ball in your hand to acquire the correct position."

"Thank you, thank you," I murmured in response.

"Yes, it takes time," she added with what I interpreted as an expression of sympathy.

Time. It always takes time.

10

Practise, Practise!

*I*nto the beginning of my third year, practising was an ongoing application of drill and sweat, frustration and persistence. In taking up the cello, I'd rediscovered the traditional meaning of the word *praxis*: "to perform (an activity) or to exercise (a skill) repeatedly or regularly in order to acquire, improve, or maintain proficiency."

Every day, I removed Daisy from her stand, wiped her down with an anti-static cloth, tightened the hairs of my bow loosened the day before, and set up my sheet music. Before touching the instrument, I performed a series of arm, shoulder, and hand exercises to warm up my muscles and joints, anointing my body thoroughly for the movements I was about to demand of it. I tried, usually unsuccessfully, to include a few moments of breath work and self-composure. Then, sitting on my wooden stool, I tuned my cello to Soundcorset or Tuner Lite, apps on my cellphone that ensured amateurs like me could begin in tune.

What was practising in music? Many articles, old and new, circulated and continued to be disseminated around the topic of practice. Of course, no two were ever in total agreement. Take, for example, these two tips on flexible bow holding in practice published in *The Strad* a century apart, the first by Arthur Broadley in 1905, the second by Simon Fischer in 2005:

In order that the muscles of the fingers, wrist, and forearm may be properly developed it is absolutely necessary that every portion of the bow should be properly practised. This cannot be accomplished in a few weeks or even a few months — it is a case of growth, and all growth is by nature a somewhat slow process.

What is the best way to hold the bow? There is no single answer to this question, since the exact bow hold changes constantly according to what you are playing. The question should be, "What is the best way to hold the bow to play what?" To play very heavily or strongly, you might grip the bow quite solidly and spread the fingers more widely to get more leverage. To play with more delicacy, or to produce a particular dolce or special feathery sound quality, you might hold the bow so that there is barely any feeling of contact at all between it and the fingers; and allow the fingers to remain a normal, natural distance apart rather then spreading them out.[1]

Was practice just the training of muscle memory? Was it only to ensure through repetition the grafting of muscle memory onto the instrument? Repetition invisibly and mysteriously established neurological connections. I marvelled at the way our brains laid down pathways for such minute body movements in each part of our hands and arms like an invisible pattern of lace filaments etched by a master embroiderer.

Dobrochna also insisted that if we could attune our ears to hear the notes internally, our fingers would gravitate and direct us to the correct placement. The body never ceased to amaze! Practice also established the repetitive rehearsing of the fingers in the perfecting of scales: first for position, for speed, for correct connections of the shoulder-elbow-hand triad, and finally, for weighting on the bow. One long bowing equaled one elasticized note per bow without a change of bow direction; two notes per bow involved the shifting from down to up bow after every two notes, then four notes per bow, then eight, then sixteen at express speed.

I practised each scale for three minutes, then five minutes; did multiple scales for three minutes, then five minutes; changed my emphasis from slow and lyrical to fast and staccato; played the scale loud, using more weighting and lower on the fingerboard; or practised softly, lightening my touch and riding higher on the fingerboard. Then I played with different bowings: *arco*, "smooth"; *pizzicato*, "plucking"; *vibrato*, "vibrating"; *détaché*, "detached"; and *martelé*, "hammered." Experts write: "Scales must never become rote repetition. It is important to emphasize a particular motion, a different aspect of playing to avoid aimless rehearsal."

The practices of sitting *zazen* (Zen meditation), daily walking, and regular routines shared by friends and colleagues were other things I thought about. Practice had already become a regular feature of my daily life, a repetitive mantra that ensured ongoing continuity and memory.

Yet more importantly for me, practice became a sacred time and place. Aside from my occasional cynicism and discouragement, I came to view practice time as hallowed and sacrosanct, an activity set apart from the rest of my day, like a daily Sabbath break. Playing within the solitude of my private space, I could experiment and relax. I swooned with Daisy in my arms in a lyrical passage, admiring my proficiency, cringed and stomped the floor when I consistently missed notes, making micro or macro errors in intonation. Never, though, would I play as well for Dobrochna, for my Lawlor or friends, as when I stepped into my zone of practice.

I tried to remain generous with myself in terms of the pace of my progress. Despite persistence and diligence, overall progress was like a long-awaited spring. I fought against my impatience over missed notes, poor sound quality, and impossible finger stretches.

Dobrochna once explained that musical memory was muscle memory and that the music must be repeated several times to become encoded. "When you learn a piece," she said, "it must become part of you. For example, I learned a Johannes Brahms trio as a student, then was asked to play it for a recital, and finally played it in a concert. So, it became a part of me that now remains within me forever."

I visualized Freud's topographical model of memory. A geological concept of layered memories, like strata of rock striations recording history.

"I thought memory was recorded somewhere in the brain, not just in the muscle," I said to Dobrochna.

"True, memory is recorded somewhere in the brain, and interconnections between the brain and muscles exist. You need to trust that, as well."

"And how was your practice this week?" Dobrochna asked me one day, a question I always heard as a prelude to a lesson.

"Progress is very slow," I replied.

"You can't speed or rush the time required for your muscles to adapt and change, for your brain to process all the sensory input, for your ears to discriminate new sound combinations, and for all this information to become integrated. Why do you think so many people try and then give up learning a stringed instrument? And I'm not only talking about adults. With the piano, at least you can play a tune and be confident your intonation will be correct, but with strings, you need to find the actual note on the fingerboard and hit it *correctly* each and every time."

No comfort there, I whispered under my breath.

And then, on another day, with a calmness I hadn't experienced yet, it happened. I played through my Luigi Boccherini *Minuet* rather well with only a few errors in intonation, at a reasonable pace, and with smoothly connected bowing.

I heard myself *perform* the piece in an artistic manner I could recognize.

Excited to show off my well-practised piece to Dobrochna, I anticipated her expression of pleasure and delight at my improvement. But alas, I once again faltered, missing notes and completely messing up. "I knew I shouldn't have said anything when we started the lesson," I muttered.

"I see the differences in your playing. You know playing in front of someone reduces your performance by at least thirty percent. That's why you need to be super-prepared whenever you have to play in front of someone. We say practice will always outshine performance."

Oh, the wisdom of teachers. Oh, the frustration of pupils.

On a Zoom workshop I attended, the Quebec violinist and creator of the "Mind over Finger" technique, Dr. Renée-Paule Gauthier, spoke about the importance of slowing down and pausing in practice. She suggested a mindful approach to practice: "If you pause, gather all your patience, give yourself a chance, and make the decision to trust yourself and see what happens when you believe you can find solutions ... you might just amaze yourself."

I suspected many friends and colleagues would be pleased to hear about this new direction in music practice.

Going to sleep that night, I wrapped my arms tightly around Lawlor. As I drifted off, I smiled as I imagined inhaling deeply, wrapping myself in a cocoon of self-trust, and playing a Dvořák cello concerto to a packed concert hall in an unknown city.

At an afternoon concert featuring the Beethoven sonatas at Koerner Hall, I almost hugged a stranger I thought was a former colleague I hadn't seen in many years. "Hi, Martin," I said, reaching forward but hesitated as I replaced my sunglasses with my indoor ones. I stopped short when I realized he wasn't Martin but his doppelgänger.

"I think you've mistaken me for someone else. My name's Thomas," he said calmly despite the near-physical assault.

We laughed and exchanged pleasantries, and I learned Thomas was a pianist. At the intermission, we sat on the outdoor patio of the music hall overlooking Philosopher's Walk on the university campus. A sense of familiarity and ease descended.

"How long have you worked as a professional musician?" I asked him. Successful artists are inevitably the envy of those who strive to make a name for themselves. I must have appeared starry-eyed.

He smiled. "You realize we solo musicians spend more time offstage than we do onstage. In other words, I spend more time practising than I do performing. As a pianist, I need to make sure a particular piece isn't only engrained in my muscles and my mind but that my fingers, tendons, and joints are also loose and lithe. I have to ensure I can sustain the physical activity and endurance required to perform a concert. Without practice, I can't count on my attention, concentration, or musical vision to take flight. In other words, if I wish to be free in my playing, I must have practised in my sleep. And even then, we know we'll never play as wonderfully as we do behind closed doors in the privacy of our little studios."

What exactly were my dreams, my musical ambition? I pondered, returning to my seat. Would I have ever wanted to become a solo musician devoting my existence to a life of practice, rehearsals, travel? Would I have been prepared to sacrifice relationships and family for dedication to a profession in the name of love for an instrument? And what about the hours of gruelling practice, the competitiveness in the early years of training, and the unrelenting inner voice of self-doubt and self-critique? And, of course, that assumed a certain innate talent recognized and nurtured from the carefree days of being a preschooler.

Dobrochna told me that she knew many young and talented students on track to become professional musicians whose verve and élan for their music dissipated as they reached university. The temptations of easier lifestyles attracted their attentions and lured them away from their musical paths.

My current motivation, energy, and enthusiasm as a cellist were completely and diametrically opposed to the enforced drills of practice I experienced as a child studying music. Piano was a diversion imposed by my parents as part of a well-rounded education. While I enjoyed the pastime, like most children, I resented the discipline imposed by my teacher and parents.

"I just wish I'd started ten years earlier," I complained one day to Dobrochna and my friends. "Not necessarily as a child or a teenager or even as a young adult. I just wish I'd started ten years earlier so I could at least be that much farther ahead and increase my chances of playing with others."

My neighbour, Susan, recommended I read *Play It Again: An Amateur Against the Impossible* by Alan Rusbridger. An erudite as well as a politically and socially connected editor of *The Guardian* in London, Alan decided to master the formidable Ballade No.1 by Chopin in the space of one year. With dogged determination and a resolute goal, he describes in his book the process of his musical challenge in detail: the lessons he took, the pianists he met, the different approaches he studied. What we learn later is that Alan played piano beforehand and was no true neophyte to the instrument.

Provocatively, Alan questioned his performance as an amateur. A high-flying executive whose year of learning was interrupted by the exigencies of his career, he was clearly a super-achiever who expected nothing less than perfection of himself. At one point, he pondered whether his herculean efforts to play the Chopin piece provided any benefits for music itself and whether he was in any way enriching the world of classical music.

As if to assuage his bruised ego, he remembered a quote from the jazz legend Charles Cooke, who writes about amateurs in *Playing the Piano for Pleasure*: "For you there is no grim grind of practising; no exhausting burden of responsibility, no fierce competition; no endless facing of audiences regardless of the condition of auditoriums, acoustics, or the state of your soul."[2]

In contrast to this innuendo of amateurs as second-class musicians, I preferred to consider the derivation of the term *amateur*. The origin of this word came from the Latin *amare*, meaning "to love," or "one who has a taste for some art, study, or pursuit, but does not practise it," from French *amateur*, "one who loves, lover."

As Steven Hough, the English pianist writes in *Rough Ideas*, his delightful collection of musings: "An amateur is not someone who is less good than a professional but rather someone for whom love overcomes obstacles — and practising is all about overcoming obstacles. In fact, many professionals could learn a thing or two about the love for music that fills the lives of so many who have other daytime jobs."[3]

While reading, I wondered why Rusbridger felt the need and desire to contribute to the canon? Why was it not enough that he set himself a self-imposed challenge? And why did he think he could outsmart all the pianists who struggled for years with one of Chopin's masterpieces? Did I detect a certain grandiosity in his musings about his potential contribution to this, his *impossible* feat?

And yet, who was I to judge? Didn't I also harbour my own fantasies of one day being able to entertain my friends and even strangers with enough musicality and sonorous persuasion to move them to tears? No modesty there!

11

Age and Aging

For most of my childhood, the house on Queen Mary Road in Montreal was inhabited by three generations: my maternal grandmother, my parents, and my sister and me, spirals of history all spinning inside one central residence.

Born in the "old country," my *bubbe* in no way resembled my parents or any of my friends' parents. The plus-sized garments my mother bought for her at Kresge's, a low-end department store, that covered her corpulent body, were in sharp contrast to the fashionable wardrobe worn by my mother. And thinning grey hair left my grandmother's scalp exposed in blotches that reminded me of salt shakers.

In her accented dialect, she spoke of such alien places as the Austro-Hungarian Empire and strange-sounding cities like Bukovina and Czernowitz. She referred fancifully to Emperor Franz Joseph I with praise and gratitude and admired the late Queen Elizabeth II, the figurehead of Canadian nationhood.

If I considered my grandmother to be from the Age of Dinosaurs, my mother, by contrast, was a model of her time. Radiant and youthful, energetic and vital, she moved through the house like a raging force. Resenting the constant comparisons and incessant questions posed by my friends — "Are you two sisters? Boy, is your mom ever hot!" — I secretly hoped I'd match her youthfulness and vitality when I, too. aged.

Despite burgeoning social movements infiltrating

mainstream culture, my mother stalwartly upheld a traditional role of housekeeper and homemaker. I once questioned
her on Betty Friedan's book *The Feminine Mystique* lying
on her bedside table. Her dismissive response — "What a
bunch of nonsense!" — left me speechless. In my low-slung
bell-bottoms and woollen poncho, wooden orange beads, and
headband, I knew it was a skirmish not worth promoting.
Instead, I left my mother to her polished silver and art-
covered walls, her tweed skirts and cashmere sweaters, and
sped off to meet my like-minded girlfriends and boyfriends.
To her credit, in her aging, my mother became liberated
enough to live with a man in a common-law relationship
years after my father's death.

Vibrant and active well into her late eighties, my mother
retained her strength and charm and all her cognitive abilities. At the age of ninety, she was gifted a trip to Spain by
my sister and brother-in-law, choosing herself to go with a
regular tour operator rather than one specializing in trips for
seniors. It was after this journey and the surprise birthday
party I hosted that her third and final bout of cancer was
diagnosed. A strong-willed and determined warrior in her
own right, my mother defied the physical aspects of aging,
living her life on her own terms, seemingly oblivious to the
passage of time.

If my grandmother was a dinosaur and my mother a
female Peter Pan determined to outsmart the aging process
by her natural vitality, then what was my ideal of an aging
woman? I wondered. How would I construct a picture of a
maturing woman in the twentieth-first century? What were
the role models outside my own maternal lineage whose
conservative life choices I'd already renounced in my youth?

Certainly, not television women like June Cleaver from
Leave It to Beaver or Mary Tyler Moore or the romantic movie
images of Marilyn Monroe or Luigia "Gina" Lollobrigida.
And what about those women in the TV commercials of
yesteryear? Where are they today? We baby boomers were
carving out new pathways in and for our time.

Today, I look at myself in the mirror and contemplate the lined face and slender body that confront me. What do I see? Who have I become? Despite the white hair, a genetic endowment from my paternal lineage, I still feel youthful. Unlike many friends, I don't suffer the typical aches and pains of aging muscles and tendons, the more critical deterioration of lungs and arteries, the unwanted rapid cellular growth of cancer. From cheaters to progressives, my eyes were the first reminder of the passage of time. Yes, there was the menopausal tornado that disrupted the hormonal balance throwing moods and body temperature into temporary disarray. And on the heels of that turbulence, the very subtle, almost imperceptible shifts, in memory and recall: "Now what was the name of that movie director? What was the title of that last book I loved? Where did I leave the documents for the meeting with the lawyer?"

"Sorry, I forgot. The joys of becoming older," I admit when asked a question I can't answer. Hiding behind my age when convenient, I simply add, "Another senior moment." My friend, Lois, balks at the use of that term. "Please, not senior. Let's say *elder*. It sounds much more radical and trailblazing!"

As an alternative, Rosie, the mother of my stepchildren whose analytic background has inducted her into the mythological realm of Jungian archetypes, claims we should refer to ourselves as the pagan daughters of Hecate the Crone. "You know, Mavis dear, we really should share with others our wisdom and intuition. Don't forget the natural cycles: birth, life, death. You and I, we're now the forebears of our years of experience. We must make sure to impart our hard-won intelligence and insight to the children and grandchildren." Spoken like Hecate herself!

Yet what about the ageism Lois claimed to be encountering in her grant proposals for her installation art and my stalwart friend, Jeffrey, was upbraiding in his requests for scientific funding at the university? Were people of a certain age no longer entitled to their pursuits of excellence and creativity? Did men and women of a certain age have to necessarily forego the pleasures, the *jouissance*, associated with youth because they passed a threshold determined by social conventions?

My patients of a certain age have described a sense of foreboding, a fear of becoming invisible, of confronting the scornful looks of a generation waiting to fill their positions and office spaces. Now I, too, was facing the tacit anxieties that have terrorized and crippled so many men and women at the thought of getting older, at being no longer glorified when saying, "I'm a baby boomer."

"It's like we're supposed to give up having fun, being silly, and all that's spontaneous and improvised," said my friend, Pat. "Who knew one day we'd become our mothers chastising the young for not seeing us as fully alive and engaged individuals?"

Sometimes I went to bed, wondering, *What is later in life? What is late? Late for what? According to whom?*

Images of the lone dahlia in our garden at the end of October, its crimson head held aloft amid the barren bushes, appeared to me. Single and solitary, it stood aloof, trying to outlast the first frost. As I strolled through the neighbour-hood ravine, I, along with other photo enthusiasts, tried to capture the explosion of gold, russet, and burgundy lining the pathway of trees — an aesthetic feast for the eyes in anticipation of the white deadness of winter.

In the catalogue of my relatives, one figure overshadows the others. In her sixty-first year, my father's younger sister attended the first day of her higher education at Concordia University. Aunt Ida was accepted into an undergraduate degree program. Four years later, in 1983, she graduated with a bachelor of arts with a major in political science.

Having grown up in poverty, my aunt never completed high school. Like her eight siblings, she was forced to work and support the family. While education was clearly valued, the necessity of putting cabbages and potatoes on the table was deemed more important.

"I want to be a better person, Mavis," she informed me on one of my few visits with her during this period of self-improvement. "I want to educate myself so I can learn what I've missed all those years raising children and being at home. With your Uncle Saulie's passing, I now have time to explore the world of ideas I always wished to do. As you know, your grandfather always stressed the importance of education."

Having never met my paternal grandfather, I only knew him by reputation through correspondence with my cousin, Mel, the family archivist. The only image of this blood ancestor I retained was a sepia photograph of a man whose steely eyes and thin lips, narrow frame, and stern expression stared out into the distance. From snippets of conversation between my cousins, I culled a composite of my grandfather as an orthodox and deeply religious man with strict standards of comportment and a sombre demeanour. He was a patriarch who sent his children to do his bidding to sustain his deeply orthodox practice. "You know, we had to go to *shul* every morning at 5:00 a.m., even in the winter months," my father often told me.

Two years later, on my next visit to Montreal, Aunt Ida exploded with excitement as she shared her progress. "Mavis, I can't tell you how excited I am about what I'm learning. History, political science, psychology!" With the jubilation and glee of a toddler taking her first steps, she grabbed my hand and led me into her bedroom. "Here, let me show you some of my books and writings."

Ceremoniously placed like coronation paraphernalia atop the quilted bedding, I saw containers of files, clips, and staples. A pile of papers like a chimney stack crowded a third of her bed. Reaching over and removing a sheaf of papers bound in a green-and-gold folder, she held out a typed essay, "Life and Mode of the Cossacks from Their Beginnings to the Present Era," and a second, "Processes and Theories in the Development of the Self."

With splotches of red lip gloss, mouth parted as a smile broke over her face, she threw her arms around me. "I'm going to graduate soon, Mavis. Oh, Mavis, Mavis," she added, repeating my name like a mantra. "Mavis, can you believe it? Me, your Auntie Ida? At sixty-five?"

Whenever I closed my eyes and pictured Aunt Ida then, I saw all five feet of her sipping coffee and conversing in her raspy voice with a group of twenty-year-olds, excited and excitable, full of ideas and life, outspoken and assertive, despite her limited formal education.

Aunt Ida continued her university education, enrolling in a master of arts program, but died at the age of seventy-one, three courses short of her degree. Her son-in-law asked the university to grant her a posthumous diploma, but the higher powers refused to comply with the request.

When the subject of later-life learning emerged in my writing, I called my two cousins, Aunt Ida's children: Judy, an immigrant to California, and Murray, a diehard Montrealer. I grilled them about their mother's decision to pursue her degree, as well as her accomplishments.

Murray proudly spoke of his mother's resolve to become a self-taught woman later in life, having to complete her high school matriculation before being accepted into the university program. With gratification in his voice, he said, "And just imagine, not only did she obtain her degree, and Judy and I get our undergraduate degrees, but her grandson, Steven, is a Harvard graduate."

From my cousins, I learned that as the oldest in her classes, my aunt was perceived as an older sister, *hip* mother, and even *cooler* grandmother to different cohorts of students with whom she interacted regularly. I discovered she excelled in her classes, being a determined and diligent learner, and heard she was outspoken, once taking the bold step to denounce a professor for his anti-Israel stance resulting in an invitation to his house for dinner. Aunt Ida remained strong-willed and strident, qualities I never knew about her as a young niece.

Shortly after my conversation with Judy, a manilla envelope appeared in the mail. My cousin handwrote a list of all the classes and paper titles from her mother's undergraduate years. A signed note at the bottom read: "Hi, Mavis, I hope this information will help you, if only, in just a little way. So glad my mom's ambitious self-improvement project will see the light of day."

My aunt never knew the impact of her educational pursuits on my own interests. Born of a generation when education was valued but not accessible or available to most women, nor to many Jewish men due to university quotas at the time, my aunt lived her life calmly maintaining the traditional lifestyle expected of her. She dreamed big, and with her daughter's encouragement, had the courage and fortitude in later life to pursue a path not taken by most women of her generation.

It has been well-documented that artists, too, continue to produce some of their best work in later life. I was heartened to discover that, at the age of ninety, Antonio Stradivari created the "Willemotte" Stradivarius of 1734, named after Charles Willemotte, a distinguished nineteenth-century collector, connoisseur, and amateur player from Belgium. Considered one of the most robust violins ever made, it was described as having an unforgettable voice: "dark, shimmery, and plaintively expressive."[1] Three years later, on December 18, 1737, Stradivari, the Italian master who raised the art of violin-making to its highest level, died.

Pablo Casals, the pre-eminent Castilian whose name will be eternally linked with cello virtuosity and in whose name International Cello Day is celebrated annually on December

29, continued to perform and conduct well into his nineties. According to Casals, the persistent vitality of an orchestra in the Caucasus composed of centenarians was a result of a zest for life and pursuit of their passion for music. He himself harnessed the aging process to his advantage and modified his interpretations to a more leisurely and reflective tempo in correspondence with his own *ritardando*. In his autobiography *Joys and Sorrows*, Casals wrote:

> On my last birthday I was ninety-three years old. That is not young, of course. In fact, it is older than ninety. But age is a relative matter. If you continue to work and to absorb the beauty in the world about you, you find that age does not necessarily mean getting old. At least, not in the ordinary sense. I feel many things more intensely than ever before, and for me life grows more fascinating.[2]

Apparently, Casals performed two Bach preludes and fugues daily in order to bless both his home and daily awakening.

How many other writers, composers, and artists whose creativity and productivity flourished well into their senior years have credited their youthful energy to their passion for work? In the field of music composition, Ludwig van Beethoven and Gustav Mahler, while young in terms of today's measures of longevity, both produced masterpieces later in their lives, as did Giuseppe Verdi, Anton Bruckner, and Emmanuel Chabrier. No doubt they were inspired by their accumulation of life experiences and their unfailing verve to communicate with the world through their music.

And how many others, in past and present times, have chosen to re-engage with an art form in later life or to engage with a completely different field of study? Recent research shows that our brains continue to form new neural networks and pattern recognition capabilities that we didn't have in our youth when we had more horsepower. In *Late Bloomers: The Hidden Strengths of Learning and Succeeding at Your Own Pace*, the journalist Rich Karlgaard has written about late bloomers, claiming that *fluid* intelligence, which encompasses the management of novel challenges and thinking on one's feet, biases the young. But *crystallized* intelligence — the ability to draw on one's life experiences and expertise, to handle setbacks and to manage expectations — is enriched by maturity and age.[3] Others suggest that varying cognitive skills rise and fall across the lifespan, a modification of the notion that critical periods are restricted to childhood and youth.

In Ari Goldman's entertaining book *The Late Starter's Orchestra*, we learn that this former *New York Times* reporter and Columbia University professor of journalism decided to reacquaint himself with the cello in his late fifties after a twenty-five-year hiatus. For his sixtieth birthday, he made a pact with himself to study, master, and perform Bach's Minuet No. 3 from *Suzuki Cello Book 3* to a crowd of 100 family and friends.[4]

I felt a certain smugness as I read the words detailing Goldman's struggles with timing and fingering, tempo and intonation. I, too, had wrestled with this piece, yet must admit that I had perfected it only weeks earlier myself. Despite my sense of bravado, I held my breath as I read about his birthday appearance onstage, cheering him on for his bravery and chutzpah.

Goldman's book is a tribute to the number of adults in middle and old age who have been successful in learning or relearning a musical instrument, even a string instrument that places high demands on all of one's faculties simultaneously. Paralleling the Suzuki method itself, which encourages musical immersion and doles out positive feedback for all minor steps accomplished along the way, his book is a testament to the power of later-life learning.

MAVIS HIMES

Late starters, to use Goldman's term, recognize that music is learned in deliberate mini-steps and requires an investment of time on a regular basis. Echoing Malcolm Gladwell's initial mantra of a 10,000-hour regimen to gain mastery over a new skill, Goldman underscores the importance of those hours.[5]

In the early to mid-twentieth century, Shinichi Suzuki had already highlighted the value of repetition, writing that ability equals knowledge plus "10,000 times." He claimed this would ensure the acquisition of a skill that could then be applied to a piece of music. Today, neurological studies describe the way nerve pathways in the brain converging to perform a task are wrapped in a myelin sheath and that each wrapping allows a specific task to be performed later and with greater ease. Suzuki reminded us of the caveat that one must make a systematic and recurring effort *with intention*, as opposed to mindless repetition.

At sixty-four, Nell Painter entered the bachelor of fine arts program at Mason Gross School of the Arts at Rutgers, the State University of New Jersey. Unlike my Aunt Ida, Painter was "reinventing herself" as an artist following her successful career as an academic. In her congenial memoir *Old in Art School*, Painter, a former professor of history at Princeton University, writes about her dream of becoming an artist in retirement. Mixing and meddling with a coterie of like-minded youth, she settled into this endeavour with complete seriousness and motivation.[6]

Yearning for artistic freedom and determined to work at a professional level, she threw herself into her project. Soon, she was devoting herself completely to her artwork, immersing herself in this new world. Despite her conscious attempts at restraint, she couldn't rein in her driving need to achieve success and receive praise. A master of fine arts from the Rhode Island School of Design succeeded her undergraduate degree, and shortly thereafter she began having shows. Currently, she is a well-heeled artist.

How many of my own friends choose to sit in classes with paints and easels under the scrutinizing eyes of a notable artist, with a vase and bowl of cherries, a nubile male or female? How many others are perusing the rocky lakefronts and trailing meadows, mountainous backcountry and off-the-beaten track trails of Southern Ontario, trying to capture a quintessential landscape in a photograph? And how many have had their works appear in local art galleries, artist co-ops, hip restaurants, and furniture shops?

Certainly, as mature adults, we bring to the table life experience, intelligence, and motivation. We recognize our inability to recapture the plasticity of mind and the luxury of time associated with youth. While examples of people with stellar achievements late in life attest to the capabilities of our brains to create new pathways and acquire new skills, we're also profoundly aware of lapses in memory, loss of acuity in vision, and persistent needs for repetitive practice.

"No, I can't learn this piece by memory," I told Dobrochna early in our history of lessons. "I simply can't do it. Too demanding."

She backed off, but two years later encouraged me to memorize a piece I wished to perform for my Ladies' Lunch group, an annual reunion of friends. "If you can memorize the notes, it'll help not only with intonation but also with musicality. Not only will you be able to hear the music in your head, it will allow you to perform in a deeper way."

Hidden inside, I knew memory wasn't totally culpable; the effort demanded of my grey matter seemed over-whelming. Mind over matter or matter over mind — that was the question.

My friends and I try to create a vocabulary to discuss this phase of our lives. I dislike the frequently used term of *reinvention*. For me, it conjures up reupholstered furniture, reused bric-a-brac, all items refashioned and remodelled. I have no desire to reinvent myself at this late stage, even if it were possible.

I feel similar discomfort with the phrase *ripening into old age*, a metaphor that conjures up mouldy peaches and smelly bananas. Even *late blooming* suggests missed opportunities and bungled first occasions.

No, for me, life is a Homeric odyssey, an inner and outer journey of exploration and curiosity, a singular adventure we each pursue. While haphazard events and unforeseen surprises, both positive and negative, may clutter and disrupt our preferred trails, we each arrive at the natural conclusion of our chosen journeys.

12

The Search for a New Cello

*I*n March 2020, I wrote in my music diary: "For the past few weeks, my body has started responding with new reactions. My left wrist, after months, has finally cleared up. Now my thumb and the base of my palm are speaking to me. I persist in my warm-ups for back muscles, shoulders, rotator cuff, arms, wrists, as advised."

"This is a very common issue," Dobrochna confirmed. "I, too, had this when I was younger, since it happens with the playing of longer pieces. Paradoxically, it requires more playing to overcome it … and we must manage this before it becomes chronic."

I was introduced to new exercises to help out such as super-slow scales to release the thumb. But how did one press down on all fingers without engaging or gripping the thumb? I could manage this on a slow scale but not when playing fast pieces. The culprit seemed to be the third and fourth positions on the cello, which meant sliding my hands down farther on the fingerboard and extending my fingers more.

Six months after my last appointment, I returned to the mint-green walls of Dr. Linda Dvali's office. "I don't want to give you another injection, so I'm going to suggest a program of physiotherapy," she told me.

I left her office with a handwritten note on a prescription pad: "Diagnosis: Left De Quervain's Tenosynovitis. Please assess and treat." I wondered why she didn't mention this diagnosis the first time but didn't have the inclination to question her methods.

A week later, I landed in the office of a physiotherapist to deal with my hand that was speaking to me once again *fortissimo*. Another series of new exercises augmented my daily routine, and within a few weeks, I returned to a pain-free existence. Thank God for physio exercises.

"I think it may be time to consider trying out another cello," Dobrochna announced shortly after my latest medical fiasco. She made this statement quietly at the end of a lesson. A simple assertion. No fanfare, no fuss. Straightforward and direct.

On the other hand, I was thrilled and overjoyed, interpreting this casual comment as a testament to my musical progress. "Really? You think so?" I asked innocently, inside feeling like a giddy girl rewarded an extra treat for being good.

"I've always felt you'd benefit from a slightly smaller cello, not three-quarters like I originally thought, but a seven-eighths size. While your hands have definitely stretched, I'm sure you'd be more relaxed, and your body more comfortable with a cello more matched to your size."

I certainly agreed with her assessment, suspecting that a slightly smaller cello would allow me to move my fingers more nimbly on the fingerboard and across the strings.

Inwardly, I also hoped a superior cello of a more suitable size would magically enhance my playing. Aside from the upgrade in quality, I fantasized improvements in tone, sound quality, agility, in the same way a skier whose proficiency on the slope might dramatically improve with more technologically advanced boots and skis. That said, I didn't foresee or anticipate what a frustrating and baffling process the acquisition of a new cello would be.

First, I noticed concerns about my relationship with Daisy. I'd already formed an attachment to this instrument in spite of her bulky frame and tinny sound, so I felt a certain disloyalty at the thought of moving to another cello, as if I were abandoning my first love. Even my friends shared my emotions. "Well, what about Daisy?" they asked. "How will she feel?"

Oh, Daisy, of course, I value you as my first partner, and naturally, I'll cherish our time together. From those first moments of "Twinkle, Twinkle" with your neck bound in coloured tape to mark my finger placement, now to Schumann's Gavotte and Bach's Bourrée, we did make music together and I so value those memories. Don't ever, for a moment, believe I'll forget all those days of exploration and communication together.

Dobrochna had already singled out a cello for me, one she'd mentioned months earlier when we'd discussed my finger challenges. This particular cello had belonged to a colleague of hers who had decided to return to a full-sized instrument with a bolder sound. Dobrochna was dubious about her colleague's reasoning and assured me this was a wonderful-sounding cello.

"It's a French cello with a rich sound. I believe it was made in the 1800s," she said matter-of-factly. "And we'll also see about a new bow that might be a better pairing with this instrument than the one you have. Let's wait and see. French cellos are spicier and bolder in their sound than Italian ones. French instrument makers tend to give the cello a palette of different tones, colours, and shades from dark to bright passing through mellow. By contrast, Italian cellos project with brightness and directness. Of course, the French are more piquant and risqué! They flaunt their colourful personalities in their sense of style and panache!"

The truth was I wasn't sophisticated enough yet to perceive these sound differences. Nor did Dobrochna need to tell me that the exchange from a beginner commercially made cello to a professionally handmade one of that vintage would be an enormous leap on multiple levels — not only sound quality, musicality, and comfort, but also finances.

As the Covid-19 epidemic descended globally and Toronto was still in partial lockdown, Dobrochna arranged for me to pick up the cello from Heinl's. She informed me that Ric would prepare everything, ensuring the cello was sanitized, and I could then keep the instrument on loan for a few weeks.

Now, more than two years after getting Daisy, I was about to make a much more informed decision. Ric met me in the tiny courtyard beside his store. First, we took care of all the required paperwork. When that was done, Ric said, "Well, take this baby home and see what you think. I'll say no more but do call me later to give me your first impressions. Dobrochna has asked me to include a bow that I think is a good match, so I included a pernambuco one I think is well suited. See what you conclude."

We said our goodbyes, and I marched over to my car parked close by and very tenderly laid the cello in the back seat. As I navigated the fifteen-minute drive home, I became obsessed about the possibility of an accident. As if transporting a newborn, I kept imagining a huge truck streaking through a red light and smashing into my car at an intersection.

Safe at home, I delicately liberated the cello from the back seat, carried it across my arms like a wedding dress, and placed it on the living room floor. Unfortunately, Lawlor wasn't home to share the excitement. Like the performance of an ancestral ritual of welcome, I found myself circling the encased instrument several times, wishing to prolong the exhilaration and suspense of this new encounter.

Finally, I approached and unzipped the case, removing my prized possession. Compared to Daisy, it felt weightless. *Ooh-la-la* ... the aged wood, a deep caramel, warm and mellow in hue. I'd been told the front, or table, of the cello was made of European spruce, while the ribs, back, and scroll were European maple, all with a varnish of golden-brown over amber.

Lifting the cello to the window, I peered into the left f-hole to find the inscription of authentication I was told to locate. And there it was in black ink in calligraphic script on a faded piece of sepia paper: "Caussin Luthier; Neufchâteau (Vosges), 1867." The name of the luthier, (instrument maker), the place of origin, and the date.

An instrument made in the year of Canadian Confederation. That was an auspicious date, one I associated with freedom and boldness. I wondered if Caussin was aware of the historical events happening across the Atlantic. Did he know that a territory was being founded and recognized officially as the Dominion of Canada? Would he have cared, even if he did know?

Before putting bow to instrument, I called Dobrochna. I needed to share my delight.

"Take your time," she advised me, trying to calm me down. "When you begin to bow, pay attention to your left hand and see how your fingers move. And notice any differences. Also, try using your old bow on the cello as a basis for comparison. See how each one feels and how the sound carries."

I hung up and ceremoniously pulled out my cello seat, placed the music stand in front of me, and held the cello in my grasp. Enfolding myself around this smaller, more petite instrument, I held her tightly — I'd already decided this cello was on the side of the feminine — and moved it slightly, swaying with my eyes closed, trying to absorb the warmth of the wood, listen to the sound of a few notes, wanting to stay in this magnificent embrace forever.

The contours and fit of the new cello were immediately obvious. No longer the extended finger stretches, no longer hitting incorrect notes with every position change. The smaller body of the cello sat naturally in front of me without my having to overextend my leg position. *She's made to measure for my body, a natural match*, I thought. Immediately, I heard the dramatic change in sound quality, felt the music's vibration against my chest, the sound resonating deep within me.

I was convinced this was what it meant to play the cello, to become a cellist, or rather, an amateur cellist. A certain confidence descended. With the improvement and ease in playing, I was more motivated. I finally understood what Dobrochna had said to me in the early days of our lessons: "Play as though you own the space in which you're playing." I was possessing and incorporating this cello into the space around me as I moved my bow back and forth across her body. We were one unit.

Of course, the thrill and excitement of the first few days with this "perfectly matched" French cello were somewhat tainted by the price. Initially, I'd requested Ric not tell me the cost so I could make a decision based solely on the musicality and comfort of the instrument. Yet I hadn't anticipated this instantaneous love at first sight, or *coup de foudre*, as the French would say.

After a few days, I returned to my practice with Daisy and felt a certain carryover from the gains made from my playing on the new cello: a certain posture and movement in body, as well as an easier dexterity in my fingers. However, the transfer was short-lived when I very quickly became accustomed to the new instrument. I found myself unable to adjust to Daisy's larger frame. Unable to play simple scales and pieces without making multiple errors and missing the notes, I became increasingly concerned about returning to a full-sized cello.

Dobrochna reiterated her initial advice. "This is a process requiring patience and research. We'll have to try out several instruments before you can choose one. Don't get too fixed on anything yet. You'll have to compare this one with others, not only for comfort but also for the sound. I know you're taken with this one, but you must let yourself explore other options." When I expressed my concerns about the price, she listened carefully. "You knew this would happen. But I understand it's a bigger jump than you anticipated."

I insisted it was nonsensical for someone of my age and level to invest in a professional-level instrument. "How many years will I have to play it? What if I get sick next year or find I have arthritis and can no longer pursue this passion of mine? It makes no sense."

"In fact, Mavis," she said, using my name for emphasis, like my mother, "I have to disagree with you here. It's exactly because you're older that we want you to take advantage of an instrument that'll maximize your playing quality and comfort. This will only help you produce a sound you can enjoy yourself without the frustration and discomfort you've been experiencing. Of course, we can find a cheaper instrument of that size, but let's see what else turns up now." Knowing I had an interest in art, she added impishly, "You can always think of it as an investment, like buying a fine piece of art for your home."

Two weeks later, I returned to Heinl's and exchanged the French cello for an English one made by Johann Nicholas Lentz, an Italian-born luthier who immigrated to London after his marriage. This cello was almost full-sized in the body, though still considered a seven-eighth, but had shorter lengths on the fingerboard. Again, it was a beautiful-looking cello of a much lighter varnish with a strong and robust sound. Physically, the cello didn't seem as aged; while the French one was made more than fifty years later, its wood appeared older and a bit more brittle.

I didn't fuss as much with this one, familiarizing myself with the body and sound. Comparatively, she was still smaller than Daisy but closer to a standard full-size. I loved the wood varnish and the fingerboard felt comfortable, as well.

Dobrochna immediately thought the French cello had more resonance. In my ear, this second cello was stronger and louder, not as rich or full of sound as the French one.

In my diary notes, *brazen* was the word used to describe the English cello, whereas *refined* was how I described the French one.

In this process of observation, I was already developing new skills. I learned to discriminate minor intonation and sound differences. I discovered how my body enfolded an instrument — my upper body, torso, and arms all adjusting differently to each instrument, for example, how it adapted to the A string. I understood that a seven-eighths cello wasn't only a reference to the body size of the instrument but also to the relative dimensions of the neck and finger-board. I realized that the bow I was given for the heavier English cello didn't work as well as it did on the French one.

A week later, Dobrochna and I met at another store, Remenyi House of Music, to explore some instruments more suited to my targeted budget. With Covid-19 mask protection, we mounted the stairs to the second floor where, in the privacy of a salon-like room, we were offered a selection of seven-eighth cellos. I tried out a few myself but felt very self-conscious in front of the saleswoman who I knew had worked as a cello teacher.

When she left us alone, I relaxed and played a few scales on the particular cello we'd come to see. While handmade in a shop, it was an imitation of an older cello. I then asked Dobrochna to try it herself so I could listen. Mesmerized by her playing, I listened with rapt attention but unfocused on the cello itself. Putting down the instrument, Dobrochna immediately launched into a commentary on the sound, the strings, and the "sticky varnish." She was clearly not impressed. I realized I was still dreaming of the French cello and not prepared to give any other instrument a chance. We left, thanking the saleswoman for her time.

"I'm not up to the task, D," I blurted out as we reached the sidewalk. "I'm not sure I can really assess a new cello. I'm really struggling here."

She smiled. "Listen, it isn't that difficult. The important

criteria are comfort, sound, texture. Of course, value and cost, too. You need to feel comfortable, first of all. And you have to take your time. Would you marry someone after just one meeting?" And she laughed as we strode down the street together. "And I have a present for you," she continued, pulling out a small notepad with "J.S. BACH, *Sechs Suiten*, Six Suites" written across the front. "Now you have something to record your impressions."

Later, I read one of the entries I wrote at that time: "I'm becoming more comfortable with the English cello, but I don't love the sound. Is this presumptuous of me? After all, it's a professional instrument." A few days after that entry, I returned the English cello and exchanged it for the French one. Immediately, I sank back into the comfort of its body, just like the first time.

Dobrochna continued her research on my behalf, locating two more instruments at another store in Toronto. "We really are limited here in Toronto. There are only the three places, and a fourth in Hamilton. Because of Covid, we can't travel around anywhere, and people specializing in this field aren't shipping instruments these days."

We met at The Sound Post, picked up another cello, and took it to the lobby of Dobrochna's apartment building where we could listen to it together. While it felt comfortable, I found the sound raspy.

"You mustn't compare. You have to move with the cello and see how you like it. This looks like a nice pernambuco bow but lighter than the one you had from Heinl's." Dobrochna's detachment didn't coincide with my rapid assessment.

After a week of playing with this commercially made Haide wood cello, I decided it wasn't for me because of the raspy sound, the lack of resonance, the cheap finish with unappealing varnish, and its blotchy stains. I returned the instrument to The Sound Post and asked the staff for other options as promised, but no response was forthcoming.

So, I returned to Heinl's where I brought home a circa-1890 French Mirecourt carved cello of a LaBolero Stradivarius design. The name was clearly impressive but, in fact, while named by the luthier, it would have been produced by apprentices from that particular atelier.

"Try this one," Ric said when I picked up the instrument from his courtyard. "You may fall in love with it, and it'll be much easier on your pocketbook."

I admired this full-sized cello with a beautiful, rich, and warm sound. My body once again writhed under the strain of its physical proportions. Although I was told it would be possible to reduce the fingerboard and neck in size to accommodate my body, I returned the cello within a couple of days.

Maybe I should adjust this last instrument, since I really did like its sound. Yet the thought of tinkering with the original seemed wrong to me, despite Ric's offer.

My head was bursting. I felt stuck and unable to settle into myself or my playing.

I began to understand Dobrochna's comments. For the professional, the acquisition of a new instrument was a monumental decision and commitment with enormous implications for one's playing. Yet for me, it had also become a consequential decision to aid my amateur practice.

A few nights later, I had a dream. In the middle of attending a concert, my late father appeared to me and said, "Mavis, you're trying to make a pair of size eight shoes into a size six. Too much tinkering never works." And he walked away.

The next day, I called Ric and negotiated a price for the French cello. The offer was accepted, and I didn't have to renegotiate a mortgage!

I called Dobrochna and informed her of my decision.

Once again, her response began with cool aloofness. "It's important to maximize your playing on a superior instrument with good sound." But by the end of the conversation, her excitement was palpable on the other end of the line.

A certificate of authentication was prepared, and once again I met Ric in the courtyard. He handed me a piece of parchment paper with beautifully scripted calligraphy detailing the name and particulars of my new instrument. "Congratulations," he said, giving me a gestural bear hug due to Covid restrictions. "There's a lot of cello to grow with and much to explore in getting to know each other." He paused, then continued. "And the next issue will be the bow to match this beautiful cello. Right now, you're likely choosing a bow because your teacher recommends it, but one day, you'll come to me and say, 'Ric, I need a bow to get a different sound from this cello.'"

I returned home with my new love. Sometimes I mistrusted my gut instincts, but generally my first impressions tended not to lie or distort. I knew I was trying to avoid the price demanded by my first choice. Yet, when I placed my new cello in front of me, she fitted perfectly as if made to measure. I didn't have to adjust or accommodate, conform or twist my body. I simply sat in a natural position and felt at peace. *This cello has come home to me.*

At my next lesson, Dobrochna brought me a long-stemmed red rose and laughed. "You're no longer fostering this instrument. "The cello's now fostering *you*."

Like the narrator of *Lev's Violin: An Italian Adventure*, a captivating book of discovery about a violin's origins by the English writer Helena Attlee, I, too, became curious about my cello's previous owners, the former stewards and guardians whose fingers, hands, and arms also played her.[1] I asked Ric if he could do some digging into my new cello's history for me. He told me she'd been bought by a Welsh luthier, a friend of his who he'd contact on my behalf. Unfortunately, this friend turned out to be less cognitively astute and no longer remembered that particular cello.

I entered a new phase of dedication of practice, since the pleasure derived from my cello was cumulative. No leaping fingers, no awkward body strains in my posture, I could relax better. More profoundly, the consistency of sound reverberations within my body felt on that first day never disappeared. My eyes filled with tears every time I tried to describe the sensation to a friend.

There was a different attitude in my practice; a certain allegiance and sense of devotion arose. I could say, *I'm a student of the cello* with a conviction I hadn't felt earlier. This was no passing whim, no capricious impulse. This was a serious passion, a commitment to myself and to this instrument with whom I was to develop a powerful bond.

I wanted to explore the range of possibilities: the elemental levels of connection, the instrument's vocal characteristics, the potential contours of sound and tone. And as I write these words, I know that at the time, I wasn't quite sure how that development would occur. Instead, I gave myself over to the budding relationship with my new cello.

Now I had to come up with a name for my new cello. What a responsibility! I'd written a book on the power of names and knew naming was a call into being and a mark of uniqueness or individuality. To realize that, one only had to think of the variety of ceremonial rites and rituals surrounding baby-naming in different cultures.

While curious, I'd never asked Dobrochna the name of her own instrument. I felt it to be too personal and intrusive a question. But one day, as she was packing up her cello to leave, I gathered up my courage and asked, "So what did you name your cello?"

"My cello's name is Rafael," Dobrochna replied with delight. "I wanted an Italian name for my Italian cello. *Rafael* means 'healer.' It took me seven months to come up with the name. And now it fits perfectly and I can't imagine another one. My other cello's name is Bertha — a German one for a German cello. She lives in my apartment in Bielsko-Biała in Poland."

I winced. My grandmother's name was Bertha. Old World, old-fashioned.

But how did one even go about beginning to name a cello? As a beginner with a commercially made cello, I couldn't imagine a serious name like the Countess of Stanlein — ex Paganini Stradivarius, the cello belonging to the late internationally acclaimed American cellist Bernard Greenhouse.

With my first cello, Daisy, I had chosen a frivolous name, a moniker that suggested levity and playfulness, a whimsical name associated with amusement. When I brought home my French cello, I decided to take my time and let the notion of naming evolve as I familiarized myself with the instrument. I wanted a French name that reflected her origins but still to have been used at the particular time she was created. While this cello was on the side of the feminine, I still needed the name to suggest the masculine traits I sensed. And I certainly had to have a serious name with more gravitas.

Eventually, I landed on Simone. A French name not uncommon in the 1800s, its etymological origin has been linked to the Greek form of the Hebrew *name* שִׁמְעוֹן (Shim'on), *meaning* "he has heard" or "the listener." For me, the name Simone represented a sacred covenant with my cello.

13

The Nature of Music

*A*fter the restorative summer break of 2020, I reunited with Simone. Like a taut elastic band, time had stretched out. In my absence, I'd temporarily forgotten her deep mellow sound, like the lush and rich taste of chocolate. My fingers were out of shape, my arms tired in spite of kayaking, and my thumb once again shouting at me — *I'm here.*

I practised in front of the mirror again. My ear had become sharper, my bow grip firmer, and my sound production even deeper. As Dobrochna had said, "You're no longer fostering an instrument. You can now grow with your own cello."

One day, I woke up hearing music in my head: Domenico Gabrielli's *Ricercar*, Anton Dvořák's *Humoresque*, and Luigi Boccherini's *Minuet*, all pieces I was learning. *Hear the notes*, Dobrochna had once said. Finally, I was hearing the notes.

In September, Dobrochna and I met over sandwiches to catch up after the holidays. Waiting for her at an outdoor café, I watched her approach. She was a portrait in colour — red linen pants, a royal blue shirt, and an orange shawl to shade her shoulders. Despite Covid precautions, we hugged each other with sideways kisses in the air.

As always, our conversation was lively and serpentine. She described her frenzied schedule in Poland, noting, "After the insulation of Covid, it was great to be in Poland where there were no restrictions. People figure they'll eventually get sick and move on with their lives."

We discussed the mask mandates still in effect in Ontario cottage country. "Lining up outside small general stores, masks were one hundred percent still in full force here," I said.

Gazing pensively at the people parading by, Dobrochna changed gears, becoming very serious. "You know, Mavis, to be an artist is to live music. It's to be committed to a life in which music is ever-present. It's hard to explain."

"I think I understand. I just happened to read something like that a few days ago in *The Strad*. This acclaimed musician, whose name, of course, escapes me, wrote, "Music is not a fashion accessory — it is a way of life.""

"Exactly."

"Being a psychoanalyst is similar. We also say it's a lifestyle, a way of being or navigating through life, more than just a profession."

"My father was a musician," Dobrochna continued. "His whole life was and still is dedicated to his music. I went to school with a focus on cello playing, then, being successful at it, I joined an orchestra. I inherited my father's fierce independence of spirit and his desire to pursue his own path no matter what the risks."

"Like father, like daughter!"

"Well, good news. I've been shortlisted for a university position. Thank you so much for helping me out with the bio and curriculum vitae statement. I'm positive it helped."

I laughed and tried not to think about the implications of this on future lessons.

As if reading my mind, she added, "Not to worry. Nothing's going to happen for quite a while. It'll be another year before they hire. Besides, I heard through the grapevine that I'm competing with an internal candidate. More likely, they'd hire an American before taking on a *foreigner* like me. Now tell me about your summer break."

I talked about my long walks down country roads in the Haliburton Highlands, kayak paddling at dusk when the lake was less crowded and the water calmer, crossword puzzles on rainy days, and stargazing in the evening. Then I mentioned the interview I was planning with her colleague and friend, Norbert Palej, a composer and faculty member in the University of Toronto's music department. She suggested I clearly inform him I was interested in a conversation for non-academics and not necessarily musicians.

Fascinated and intrigued by the ability of composers to encapsulate a feeling, a mood, a landscape, I wondered how Antonio Vivaldi captured the mercurial volatility of *The Four Seasons*? How did Christos Hatzis mesmerize his audiences with *Constantinople*? And what inspired Joseph Haydn's *Surprise Symphony* or Hector Berlioz's *Symphonie fantastique*? For sure, inspiration and output didn't come without concerted effort.

Upon returning home from lunch, I pulled out a CD that Dobrochna had given me when we first started lessons. Staring at the stylized Photoshopped picture of my glamorous teacher filling half the cover, I tried to decipher a thickly squiggled line of green-and-burgundy script, eventually decoding it as "Mexico." Underneath in bold block capitals was "Voyages."

Dobrochna's musical travels had landed her in different ports of call: Poland, Paris, Mexico City, Baltimore, and Toronto. With this gesture of a gift, I'd wanted to believe Dobrochna had invited me into her musical orbit so I, too, could become part of her journey and she a part of mine.

I'd listened to the CD, the melodies of Polish and Mexican composers so foreign to my unsophisticated ears, and had tried to sustain focus but was unsettled by the unfamiliar combinations of notes. Years of concert attendance hadn't fully modified my listening discomfort for ultramodern music. On first listening, the music remained inaccessible to me despite my increased attendance at Toronto concerts by Esprit Orchestra, Soundstreams, the New Music Festival, and 21C. While my enjoyment of this music had improved, my ears still couldn't easily accept the cacophonic tones, atonal phrases, and brash rhythms. I regarded myself as a neophyte in the world of the learned patrons with their savvy nods and arched eyebrows, their stormy applause and unrestrained praise.

Recalling my initial attempts at listening to Dobrochna's CD once, twice, three times, I knew it wasn't an easily accessible recording. It required my full attention. Like the inability to sustain an unremitting focus and concentration required for mindful meditation, my monkey mind wouldn't or couldn't relax into the unfamiliar chords and obscure harmonies. My body resisted, my ears pulling away from the tension in the music. Perhaps I simply wouldn't be able to participate in this voyage with my teacher, after all.

Back then I'd put the CD away. On another occasion, I'd pulled it out but had decided to put it aside again. I'd wanted to avoid another encounter with what I'd perceived as my listening limitations.

Yet, when I returned from lunch that day, two years later, I became curious again and wished to see what I could and couldn't hear in the composers who were once so important to my teacher.

So, I plucked out the thin booklet that accompanied the CD, the same image of my striking teacher replicated on the outside as on the disc cover. Carefully, I read the notes on the artists: two different pianists and the cello played by Dobrochna. On the first page, I saw the dedication in three languages: *Moijor podgriotr: Weronite i Andrggejovi / to my parents, Veronika and Andrzej / a mis padres, Weronika y Andrgej*. I knew Dobrochna's mother had died almost five years earlier of cancer and that she'd been a teacher of Polish literature. I noticed the tribute written by her most recent teacher, mentor and friend, Shauna Rolston, under whose guidance Dobrochna had pursued her postdoctoral studies. It was then that I realized that her father, himself a jazz musician and teacher, was one of the performing pianists.

Listening to the CD this time, I paid attention to the synco-
pated rhythms of swing jazz on one particular piece of her
father's entitled *Spring Impressions* and found myself transported by the lyricism and mellowness of the piece *Aria* by
the Polish composer Kazimierz Wiłkomirski — the comings
and goings of the townspeople in Slovakia or Croatia, the
ascents and descents, the pauses of a stroll through neigh-
bourhoods, sipping coffee off a major artery, watching locals
carrying their affairs. I recognized the composer Witold
Roman Lutosławski whose sinister-sounding piece was
written in honour of a Polish musicologist and critic. The
varying rhythms and tones transported me to the mountains
of that region.

As a surprise birthday present to my stepdaughter, I'd
gifted her with a hiking trip in the Tatra Mountains. For a
fortnight, we hiked up and down the Carpathian slopes. On
one occasion, we thought we'd avoided the torrential rains
and flash flood of an oncoming storm only to see the sun
eclipsed by dark altostratus clouds that forced us to seek
shelter. Rushing to get to the nearest pit stop, we managed
to reach a place where we holed up with crowds of other
hikers and watched the storm pass over, sheets of rain buck-
eting down.

Now, as I listened to the dark melodic line of the cello
increase in tempo on Dobrochna's CD, I imagined rapid
clouds passing over. *Shall we try again or wait inside? To wait
or not to wait? To go or not to go?* Indecision soon gave way to
certainty as the music offered the gentleness of touch, the
possibility of an opening, safety, grounding — Lutosławski's
Grave: Metamorphoses for Cello and Piano. Yes, the possibility
of going out and braving the elements. I visualized myself
splayed out on a mountaintop of the Tatra where, under a
Polish sun, I experienced the euphoria of nature's splendour
from the summit. This was followed by Piotr Moss's *Pleinte*,
a piece reminiscent of repose for the souls of the dead. A

solemn requiem with windings, meanderings, bindings of sound.

I was pleased to discover I could appreciate the daring combinations of sounds, the contrasting musical moments, and the very current musical language of Moss. My ears no longer needed to retreat in flight from the bending sounds of the cello, the melting of strings from one to the other. Simply put, I wasn't as intimidated by the music this time around.

What is it about music that stirs the soul and alters our moods so readily? Tears inevitably swell in my eyes when I hear Yo-Yo Ma and Emanuel Ax play the first movement, *allegro non troppo*, of Johannes Brahms's Sonata for Cello and Piano, No. 1, Opus 38, or Leonard Cohen sing "You Want It Darker." I'm overtaken by the sounds emanating from these fellow creatures who can lace my world with tenderness and joy, heartbreak and disconsolation. Brought to a realm of surrender, I can only listen and allow the music to do its bidding with my nerve endings, sensory organs, and emotional centre.

Some, like Plato, say that music brings us into contact with greatness and leaves traces of that greatness as permanent impressions. In those rare moments, he maintains, we may enter the kingdom of the divine.[1] He also warns us that abandonment to music's immense power can be destructive and corruptive, therefore we have to be wary of its potential.[2]

Others, like psychoanalyst Anthony Storr, writing in the late twentieth century, suggest that music resonates with our inner experiences, giving form and shape structure and coherence, to something beyond words.[3] Still, others write of music's healing and calming powers. Yet music's potency remains enigmatic. Even Sigmund Freud, one of the greatest thinkers of the twentieth century, found music too inaccessible to understand. With his extensive essays on painters, writers, and sculptors, he couldn't wrap his mind around the underpinnings of music.

What is it about music that can alter our moods so readily? Why are we drawn to certain music? What is it that attracts some people to jazz or blues, others to hard rock and heavy metal, and still others to the Indigenous sounds of world music?

Armed with a barrage of questions, I met for lunch with the Polish composer Norbert Palej. Under the high ceilings and bright sunlight of the plant-based restaurant Planta, an inviting spot in Toronto's Yorkville where it was possible to have a conversation without being drowned out by noise, Norbert and I hugged each other in greeting. We'd already shared a stage, along with other performing artists, at an interdisciplinary conference I'd organized years earlier on psychoanalysis and the arts. Following that event, I'd also invited Norbert to be a guest interlocutor with me at a workshop entitled "For the Love of Music" for a group of psychoanalysts. We hadn't seen each other in years but managed to pick up conversation easily. "I'm still wondering about that age-old question on the power of music and the genius of composers like you to produce such magical works," I opened.

Previously, I'd suggested to Norbert that we were first introduced and exposed to *sound* within the interior world of our mother's belly from the time of conception, the sonority of this primary landscape resonating in the mother's heartbeat and in the other physiological systems of the mother's bodily rhythms.

"And then we're bathed in the mother tongue of what the French psychoanalyst Jacques Lacan calls *lalangue*, that very first orchestra of sound shared in a common awakening of communication between mother and infant," I continued, reminding Norbert of the primacy of language and the musical landscape that surrounded the human voice.

"That must contribute to its power. Those early cooings and babblings followed by those first primal words. As a psychoanalyst, I agree with those who say that music, being non-representational or beyond words, brings us closer to the unconscious."

Norbert nodded. "And I'd add that I'm convinced that ninety percent of my compositional work occurs at an unconscious level and is then 'cleaned up' and fine-tuned by the conscious mind that applies certain rational principles to make it more clean-cut and succinct."

I smiled and took a sip of Pinot Grigio. "And what about the whole business of meaning in music? What can you say about that? I mean, coming out of a concert or recital, some people will say, 'I understood that piece of music,' which suggests music is capable of triggering meaningful associations and impressions. And then, if music touches people in similar ways, doesn't that hint something of a universal effect? For example, I'll often agree with a friend as to whether a piece of music was happy or sad, uplifting or depressing. And yet, the same music can also trigger very different emotions in us. I always think it's a result of familiarity with a piece and all our unique extra-musical associations we may have to it."

"Don't forget that musical taste hugely depends on our lived experience, our cultural background, and what we grow up with, as well," Norbert said, waving a fork at me for emphasis. "That means we can only search for general tendencies and must be ready for far-reaching exceptions based on human nature's beautiful complexity.

"I agree that we composers know how to bestir others, exploiting their emotions. We can choose to raise or lower blood pressure, create tension, or to calmly restore a feeling of balance. We can even alter one's expectations by setting up a seemingly predictable pattern." Laughing, he continued. "After all, we're manipulators and puppeteers. Don't you agree? Haven't you felt the power of our magic to create a mood, one that makes you want to weep and another to tear out your hair?" Then, becoming serious again, he added, "For me, music will always escape mathematical predictability, so we can only talk about musical *tendencies*."

What remained so powerful for me was the personal source of inspiration Norbert described: the persistent music swirling inside, the ability to hear music as a language that spoke to him through its modulations, melodic leaps, and rhythms, the way mathematicians read formulae.

"It's uncanny," Norbert ventured as we finished lunch. "When I trust the creative process to dominate and allow sleep to take dominion over my rational mind, then music turns to speech and I perceive its events as words and sentences, and I understand them like a message, not just a musical structure. And when I wake up, I inevitably can't necessarily reconstruct this so-called meaning, nor do I believe it's the discovery of some universal truth. Instead, I'd say I've managed to uncover the meaning for myself and within myself ... at least within this particular time and place."

Returning home, I pondered Norbert's comments and the interface between our worlds of verbal language and the language of music, the conscious and the unconscious. Despite his commitment to musical rules that determine structures in compositions, Norbert agrees that musical inspiration percolates in that cauldron of the unconscious with its intrusion of the irrational and the mysterious, and that it requires, even demands, a "letting go of the controls commandeered by our egos" in order for a musical piece to fully emerge.

I also thought about the complex web of our colliding internal maps — the verbal and the musical. No wonder people felt drawn to a belief in a supernatural being capable of masterminding such an intricate labyrinth of criss-crossing pathways.

In the fall of 2020, still under the public restrictions and guidelines of Covid-19, I created a music course for myself online. I wanted to learn everything about music, to take it all in as if I were inhaling the full fragrance of a bouquet of roses and not just that of a solitary bloom.

Dobrochna had encouraged me to expand my knowledge base of musical theory. So, as a starting point, I signed up for a course at the Royal Conservatory of Music. For the next eight weeks, I placed notes on music paper and in my exercise book; read about ties, triplets, and transpositions; and studied the circle of fifths, harmonic intervals, and chord progressions. All of that was a reminder of my early days of piano studies.

Then I meticulously watched the lecture series given by Leonard Bernstein at Yale University in 1973. He offered six talks on *The Unanswered Question,* a title inspired by a composition of the same name by another Yale alumnus, the U.S. composer Charles Ives. In the first lecture, a young Bernstein, with his elfish smile, wavy black hair, and twinkling eyes, challenged the audience to reconsider the question posed by that piece of chamber music written in 1905 for string orchestra, solo trumpet, and four flutes. The provocative Ives had claimed he was attempting to capture the enigmatic nature of human existence with its myriad of riddles and dilemmas. But what exactly was the question that remained unanswered, I wondered when I first tuned in to the online lectures.[4]

"Music is the universal language of mankind," Bernstein said, echoing the words of Norbert, strutting across the stage in his black turtleneck and tapered pants. "And universality implies likeness and diversity," he added, referring to the vast number of different family languages with their common sets of rules. And from the introductory comments to the final lecture in which he spoke about "the poetry of the earth," Bernstein compared and contrasted the language of music and human language, arguing for the equivalences between notes and letters, scales and alphabets, movements and sentences. I was transfixed by the lectures, remembering my days as a graduate student trying to understand the mechanics and complexities of our speech.

Meanwhile, in my actual cello lessons, I still struggled with the banal concern of loosening my thumb, a digit that persisted in coiling itself around the fingerboard for dear life without letting up pressure. Simone improved my finger placements and shifting, but somehow hadn't been successful yet in helping me relax the vice grip of my thumb. A new program of thirty minutes to relax my thumb ensued.

"You can't advance technically until your muscles and fingers are ready to advance," Dobrochna reiterated like a refrain.

I understood the feeling as I continually battled to attain the standard of playing I set for myself. Perhaps more lessons in patience and humility should also be added. So, I wrote an email to my granddaughter who was living abroad:

> My cello learning is such an interesting journey. As I navigate the process, I've become so aware of my own tendencies, and not always the best ones: impatience, perfectionism, and moodiness. I'd been feeling quite good about my playing for a few days. Then I had a lesson in which I played a new piece. Of course, it needed a lot of work. Despite all the helpful tips and comments of my teacher, I still felt deflated. There is always something to add or improve or learn. This journey is never straightforward. Yet the love and feelings of satisfaction when I play a piece, even when it's not "perfect," is so very satisfying.

I told Dobrochna about a 1957 recording of the cellist Gregor Piatigorsky performing William Walton's Viola Concerto that I'd watched. His fingers danced up and down the strings like water nymphs, gliding, sliding, fluttering.

Like all professionals, Piatigorsky made sure his finger placements never failed. "His long, straight fingers were so easily and well placed on the higher positions," I said to Dobrochna.

"Yes, seventh position, or more accurately, thumb position, will take as long to learn as the lower positions," she remarked.

But when will I ever master the lower positions? I wondered.

I watched a YouTube video of Amanda Forsyth, the Canadian-born cellist, and Pinchas Zuckerman, her violinist husband. They spoke about the relationship with their instruments, with music, and with each other. At one point, they mentioned vibrato, the technique of pitch fluctuation by rocking the hand and wrist. Amanda claimed it was used in order for the listener to be moved, whereas Pinchas asserted it had more to do with playing well in order to produce a good sound.

I asked Dobrochna when I could start learning vibrato. "Later," she said. Period. No discussion.

For me, vibrato represented the next major hurdle in progress. I read that it was typically introduced only after four or five years of playing and that it shouldn't be started until the student played perfectly in tune.

Will I ever play with perfect intonation? I thought. *Will I ever be able to play vibrato?*

I watched multiple interviews with the next generation of mid-career cellists who had already made names for themselves on the international scene — Alban Gerhardt, Jean-Guihen Queyras, Alisa Weilerstein, Johannes Moser, and Gautier Capuçon, along with the musical titans Steven Isserlis, Mischa Maisky, and superstar Yo-Yo Ma. And if I might be so bold to recommend some music, I suggest listening to Capuçon's playing of "Hallelujah" by Leonard Cohen or "Amazing Grace" in which vibrato, seventh position, and singing bowings can be heard.

And for those in a mood for a very schmaltzy and intensely passionate cello experience, I propose watching the YouTube video of Stjepan Hauser of 2Cellos duo fame performing solo *Alone, Together* during Covid at Arena Pula in Croatia. Garbed in black tuxedo, white shirt with black cufflinks, black tie, a symbol of respect and dignity, and black shoes, Hauser performs in this ancient arena, with its empty stones, imperial columns, birds circling the open arches, as we witness the ancient property of music as a healing art recorded during the pandemic. Seen from an aerial view, the speck of a solitary figure is telescoped to the old port, the town square, and the brown-and-grey grass surrounding a kingly statue of a lion. The cello's sound reverberates with peace, hope, yearning, and longing, the tunes familiar and popular: Karl Jenkins's *Benedictus*, J.S. Bach's "Air on the G String," and arias from Italian operas.

For Hauser's finale, his cello with orchestral accompaniment croons the melody of "Nessun dorma" ("Let no one sleep"), the aria from Giacomo Puccini's opera *Turandot*, made famous by Luciano Pavarotti, while workers, their faces shielded from the transmission of infectious agents by protective coverings, begin one by one to remove their Covid masks in a sign of optimism and faith in the future. Haunting and moving, we see the human spirit demonstrate its strength in the face of adversity.

Under the shade of an umbrella tucked away in a corner of a local patio pub, I spoke with the now-septuagenarian Moshe Hammer. Slight in frame, his thinning grey hair in contrast with his suntanned face, twinkling eyes, and a generous smile, this renowned violinist had agreed to chat with me about The Hammer Band, his charitable organization. I was struck by the energy his manner embodied and the message he expounded.

"Life is music, everything is music," Moshe told me. "We breathe music, we inhale music. And do you know why this is so? It's a question I ask little children." He looks directly into my eyes, pausing for a moment before continuing. "It's because music is vibration and everything is vibration. The pulsing and throbbing, the humming and murmuring, the drumming and buzzing, droning and reverberating of our world and all that it contains within it."

A successful soloist and orchestral and chamber musician, the Hungarian-born Canadian-Israeli violinist has brought his exuberant passion and enthusiasm for music to The Hammer Band. Founded in 2007, the band established itself under the slogan "From Violence to Violins" with a mission of bringing music, and in particular string instruments, to the underprivileged and impoverished inner-city school children of Toronto. Today, "Changing Tunes, Changing Lives" has replaced the earlier mantra.

I marvelled at how this elfin-like man with an abundance of drive has managed, along with his cadre of eight teachers, to successfully expose hundreds of children to the vibrations of music. "Just prior to Covid," Moshe informed me, "we reached more than a thousand children in forty-one schools. And since the pandemic began in March 2020, we've been working online with children in after-school hours. We're hoping to be back in schools in another year when we can see children during their regular school hours. We know the overall and far-reaching benefits of music — socially, emotionally, intellectually."

In the late 1970s, the Canadian Association of Music Therapists was founded, bringing cohesion to a discipline that had practitioners such as Norma Sharpe in Ontario and Thérèse Pageau in Quebec as far back as the mid-1950s. But it took many years for the profession of music therapy to become acknowledged and recognized for its impact in the treatment of children and adults with neurological disorders or mental health issues to be better appreciated then. During my postgraduate psychology studies at the University of Toronto in the 1970s, I was already aware of language and its structures and development as well as the intersection between language and music. And then I met Billy.

14

Billy

*A*s a doctoral student in psychology in the late 1970s, I was interested in developmental psycholinguistics, especially the acquisition of language in infancy. I was trying to answer such questions as "What made language develop?" "How did a mother's speech patterns affect the emerging words and phrases being uttered by their infants?" "Did it make a difference, and if so, how?"

My dissertation revolved around the unfolding of language patterns during the first years of life. In an old house on the University of Toronto campus, I observed the interactions of mothers with their infants in a carpeted room with oversized batik cushions and three objects: a ball, a teddy bear, and a book. One by one, I videotaped proud mothers playing with their firstborns, recording all of the speech acts shared in that intimate space.

After completing my doctorate in the spring of 1978, I graduated with the credentials to begin my career as a clinical psychologist specializing in work with children. My interest in language landed me a position as a language therapist in a children's preschool mental health clinic. And it was there, in the fall of 1978, that I met Billy, a five-year-old with auburn hair, a shower of freckles, and when revealed, a smile that traced an arc from cheek to cheek. His hearing was intact, but he wouldn't speak.

Baffling professionals with his condition, Billy was finally diagnosed with selective mutism. The lack of neurological evidence and the occasional rantings and unleashed fury when unwanted demands were placed on him confirmed this initial tentatively assigned determination. His medical team members concluded there was nothing more they could offer. Perplexed by this feedback, Billy's parents sought out psychological help on the assumption that their son's mutism was a psychodynamic issue requiring a different approach. And so it was that Billy ended up in House Five of Thistletown, a Toronto day program for little boys and girls with behavioural and emotional problems.

At the bottom of my box of mementoes from my early years of work with children lies a photograph of Billy dressed up for Halloween in what today would be considered a politically incorrect costume. Garbed in a makeshift Indigenous costume, he sports a feather attached to a red bandana carefully folded around his forehead. His face painted with stripes of yellow, red, and black, hands clasping a bow and arrow, he stares at the camera, at the person standing behind the lens asking him to remain still, to pose, to allow himself to be photographed for posterity.

I wondered what he was thinking then, this little boy with matchstick arms and legs, coerced to respond positively to such an innocuous demand. Was this one more gesture he could choose to disdain or refuse, like the constant demands to speak? Did his forced smile reflect a certain resistance he might have been experiencing?

By the time I met Billy, he'd been attending the Thistletown program for three months. I was introduced to him by speech pathologist Jack, a short, stocky man with thick black-framed glasses, twenty years my senior. Jack informed me of his work to date with Billy, his methods of working with the boy, and the advances he'd made.

I was forewarned about the painstakingly slow progress that awaited me as well as the importance of establishing an initial bond. As a novice professional, I was excited, my trepidation offset by the challenge. I was still naive enough to think I could be the one to have a breakthrough, that I could make a difference in this little boy's life, opening a new path for him to follow, unshakable in the belief in my own omnipotence to solve problems and create solutions.

Billy eyed me like a wolf scrutinizing a potential captor or menace from afar. As I allowed him to choose some toys for our session in the basement playroom, he kept his physical distance. My first and only mission was to build a relationship with him and create a bond of trust no matter how long that took.

However, my bold confidence and self-assurance swiftly melted as I heeded Jack's advice to take one step at a time. Over the weeks, I recognized small cues, mini-signposts of connection. While I might speak punctuating my speech with an exclamation, declarative utterance, or upon the rare occasion, a rhetorical question, Billy showed little affect except for the occasional behavioural response: a smile, a frown, a pointing gesture.

One day, I decided to bring in a tape recorder with some music tapes. Not knowing what might appeal to Billy's taste, I asked Mary, the house mother, to suggest some discs for me. I tried the popular children's music of the times — The Chipmunks, tunes by Sharon, Lois & Bram, and Raffi's "Baby Beluga." Each day, Billy watched me select a tape and place it in the machine, quizzically raised his eyebrows, and then returned to a storybook, marbles, building blocks, or whatever object engaged his interest on that particular day. By that point, I tried to draw him into a conversation, hoping I might hit the one question, the one phrase, that might unlock his silence.

Instead, Billy continued pointing with one of his skinny arms to whatever he desired, refusing to engage or else throwing out one of the words from the limited vocabulary he employed to obtain the object of his request: "Want … book … ball …" Gesture was the lexicon Billy inhabited, signing for his demands.

One day, I decided to bring in Richard Strauss's 1896 masterpiece, a tone poem entitled *Also sprach Zarathustra*, inspired by the words of Friedrich Nietzsche. Strauss had published some of the philosopher's words into the score: "For too long we have dreamt music, now let us awake. We were nightwalkers. Now let us be daywalkers."

The music begins with "Sunrise," a short brass fanfare made famous by Stanley Kubrick's film *2001: A Space Odyssey*: first, a double low C on the double basses, contra-bassoon, and organ followed by a musical announcement of three notes, C, G, C, played by the trumpets and accompanied by drums.

To me, it was a wake-up call, an appeal to being and to beginnings, the breath of life. As Billy listened to the tape, his face lit up and he smiled in his inimitable way, his face transformed. Pointing to the tape, he said, "Again, again."

Attempting to get him to say more, I asked, "What do you want, Billy?"

He repeated, "Again, again."

Once more, I restated my question, adding a second. "What is it that you want again and again?" Like the mothers in my doctoral research who naturally expanded on the words and phrases of their children's monosyllabic demands in order to embellish their budding language skills, I tried to encourage Billy to add to his phrase.

Much to my utter amazement, he responded with "I want more music. I want that music."

Containing my complete shock at his sentences, I replayed the tape and observed as he listened attentively with his whole body in rapt concentration, arms folded across his bony chest. When the tape was finished, I spoke a little about the music, about how we wake up in the morning and make our first steps out of bed. "It reminds *me* of when I get up in the morning, when I hear or see something new that catches my attention. What about you, Billy?"

"I like it. No ... I love it."

On that day, Billy took his first steps forward with spoken language outside his home, potentially opening up his world to a larger one that could include others, and perhaps a possibility to engage with the other boys and girls in his preschool program.

I knew Billy's progress would be slow despite this single breakthrough. Unfortunately, I never got to find out more, since I accepted a position as a full-time child psychologist at another mental health clinic.

But on that day, when Billy uttered his first words, I experienced music's ability and potential to awaken a dispirited soul. Music could be introduced to reach those locked into a private world of grief and pain to lift a suffering spirit.

Back then, Oliver Sachs hadn't published his book *Musicophilia: Tales of Music and the Brain* yet, Daniel Levitin hadn't produced his research in *This Is Your Brain on Music: The Science of a Human Obsession*, and Aniruddh D. Patel hadn't written *Music, Language, and the Brain*, all of them detailing the links between music and language and the comparative research studies from linguistics, cognitive science, music cognition, and neuroscience, all supporting critical connections in the music-language interface.[1]

Music's value in the treatment of adults or children with neurological disorders wasn't fully appreciated in the 1970s. Today, though, music therapy has become a powerful tool in academia and the clinical realm to deal with many conditions.

15

Duets

A medical issue requiring surgery arose unexpectedly toward the end of my third year of cello lessons: a very early diagnosis of breast cancer picked up on a routine mammogram. Because of my strong family history of breast cancer, I wasn't shocked, just annoyed. Having worked extensively in the field of psychosocial cancer care, I was well informed about my diagnosis and the likelihood of a positive prognosis. Early detection spared me any concerns in that regard. However, I still had to subject my body to the intrusive measures of surgery — nodal biopsies around my armpit — and radiation. I was told I had to take at least a month off playing the cello.

"I'll lose all of my recent gains," I moaned to Dobrochna.

In her wise way, she reassured me. "It's always good to take a break. Things can settle. You'll see. You're too impatient, Mavis."

"But you know my mantra — 'time is precious.' I don't have unlimited time ahead of me."

A successful lumpectomy and a smooth recovery allowed me to return to the cello a month later as anticipated. I knew radiation at the end of the summer wouldn't interfere with my playing, so I was free to move forward.

Forty days after surgery, I took out Simone, my bow, my music chair, and my music stand to focus on my right arm. Just bowing — slowly, *very* slowly. I breathed, listened, and heard, experimenting with cross-bowings on open strings and using only my right arm — *largo, moderato, allegro, vivace*. After fifteen minutes, I added my left arm to the fingerboard and heard Simone come alive, sing to me, with me, as I played *my* cello. When I wrapped myself around Simone, I experienced a newfound sense of unity, sitting in front of my cello mirror and seeing myself playing the cello.

A month later, I resumed lessons. Given the warm weather, Dobrochna and I had a live session in the backyard after months of Skype ones. Cardinals and sparrows flitted above. We arranged our instruments out of the sunlight and began to play duets, pieces I'd started prior to the hiatus of surgery. Struggling through my notation errors, we played through a few times. Then, inviting Lawlor to listen to us, I introduced the music as if this were an actual performance.

"We're about to play three pieces by Friedrich August Kummer, a Romantic composer who wrote many cello duets," I explained to my husband.

Lawlor leaned back in his seat as I inhaled and cued Dobrochna to commence. We fell into a rhythm, my teacher with her musical soul and me. I swayed slightly as I lengthened my bow strokes and attempted to draw out as long a sound as possible. Tears filled my eyes as I floated with the music and sensed vibrations of Simone deep inside me. *Cantilena*: a chanting, lilting tune. *Andante*: a relatively slow-paced tempo.

Lawlor applauded. Did I imagine he had a dewy-eyed expression?

After another two-week summer break and a repair on the cello's bridge, Simone and I reunited. She sounded amazing. The intensifying resonance I experienced made me smile and kept me satisfied — definitely another restorative break. While my fingers weren't quite as nimble initially,

I was more focused with more exacting concentration on the quality and details of my playing.

I told Dobrochna I wanted to expand my horizon by playing with others, sensing a need to break out of the confines and seclusion of my practice room. "What about pairing me with another musician?" I asked tentatively at the end of a lesson. "After these three years, I'm ready to expand my reach a bit. I'm not sure about an amateur orchestra, but I might enjoy a duet or trio."

"Great idea!" Dobrochna concurred excitedly. "Let me think about this and see who I might consider a suitable match for you."

In the meantime, Dobrochna suggested I listen to Yo-Yo Ma and Emanuel Ax, an outstanding cello and piano partnership with a decades-long history. "Why don't you see if you can compare the style of Brahms, a Romantic composer, with Beethoven, a Classicist, on the margin of Romanticism. Or just listen to the phrasing of their music."

As I waited for Dobrochna's response, I took matters into my own hands and approached a neighbour. While my experience with another neighbour had been aborted abruptly due to emerging differences in expectations, I decided to ask Susan, a retired lawyer, who had emboldened herself to return to piano studies after her retirement. Fully aware her piano skills surpassed mine on the cello, we decided to give it a try, anyway, agreeing this could be an enjoyable, no stress experiment for both of us.

On the appointed afternoon, I packed up Simone, my music stand, sheet music, and rosin, then trundled down the street to Susan's house with its painted rose-on-white brickwork. When I knocked on the door; Susan and Miranda, her new kitten, greeted me.

After ceremoniously setting up and tuning, organizing the seating arrangement, and finalizing the tempo, we each took a deep breath and made contact with our instruments. With great trepidation and heightened nerves, we bumbled our way through a Beethoven minuet and a Bach gavotte with several repetitions.

While we were playing, I noticed Miranda had jumped into a large cardboard box. A sign of displeasure or disappointment? "She must be trying to tune us out," I joked.

"Oh, she does that all the time," Susan quipped.

I wasn't convinced about that, figuring the kitten was giving us her feedback.

After a few trial duo sessions, Susan decided she wanted to focus more diligently on her own repertoire, feeling our joint playing would take her away from her own musical goals. I suspected she wasn't ready to spend time with someone so clearly below her level of playing.

Today, Susan does violin-piano duets with her new partner, and we joke over coffee about our preliminary attempts to make music together, thinking we might try again another time.

"Perhaps it would be better if you played with a professional pianist for a few sessions," Dobrochna said after I shared my forays into duet playing. "You'll learn rhythm, how to listen to the other's instrument, and what to listen for when playing with others. That way you can benefit from someone's professional expertise."

Dobrochna arranged for me to play with Asal, a colleague of hers with whom she shared the stage at Toronto's Aga Khan Museum in a program of Persian-inspired music. When the concert commenced, Asal, a petite woman with jet-black hair and carnet lips, stepped out of the wings draped in a black outfit with a flowing skirt.

That Sunday afternoon, Dobrochna and Asal played Gabriel Fauré's melodic *Elegy for Cello and Piano* in addition to some other compositions for voice and clarinet. After the concert, Dobrochna introduced me to Asal, the other performing musicians, and Reza Bali, the Iranian-American composer of one of the pieces.

"I'd be delighted to have a rehearsal practice with you," Asal had written in response to my previous email request for a meeting. "Rehearsal practice" sounded grander than simply "playing together," especially when I was still mastering the early Suzuki books.

Lost in the underground parking of Asal's condominium, my spatial skills forever being challenged, I arrived frazzled and tense at her front door. With a warm welcome, she assured me it was complicated, letting me off the hook for what I knew to be my own ineptness at directions.

I entered an immaculate condo of contemporary decor, the black grand piano contrasting against the white walls. Despite my initial reservations, I'd decided to capitalize on this opportunity for learning. Putting aside, as well as I could, the internal censors forever reminding me to "play perfectly," I was determined to accept the inevitability of intonation errors and rhythm glitches.

Before we started, I still felt compelled to blurt, "Of course, Dobrochna has stressed the importance of playing through a piece, but I know my errors throw me off and I hesitate to continue, but I'll persist. Just giving you a heads-up."

"Yes, yes, let's try to see how it goes," Asal concurred, clearly comfortable in her own abilities to play and take charge. "Just try to relax, take a few breaths, and we'll begin."

I followed her advice, inhaled deeply, planted my feet, and opened my toes wide within my stockinged feet, gently and calmly anchoring my bow on the strings.

"A cue, please," she whispered as I was about to start.

Inhaling once more, I glanced in her direction and set my bow.

The first piece we tackled was Dvořák's 1894 *Humoresque*, a whimsical composition well known in the piano-and-string repertoire. Played with a light touch, this piece depicts a romp in the forest alternating with the more serious threats of an approaching storm. At least that was the image with which I'd been working as suggested by a musician whose tape Dobrochna had sent me. For contrast, we moved into the 1887 *La Cinquantaine* (*The Golden Wedding*) by the French composer Jean Gabriel-Marie, a lyrical piece described as an air on an ancient style.

I began playing and was immediately reminded of the difference between solo versus duo performance. The addition of another instrument introduced melody with harmony. The resonance in sound multiplied exponentially for me, as did the transparency of my mistakes. The piano was an unforgiving partner; it didn't let one get away with anything.

After several reiterations filled with errors in tonality and tempo, the music began to sound better as I followed Asal's instructions about the dynamics, tempo, and rhythm. We continued to play, and I relaxed over time. The pressure to perform correctly shifted imperceptibly to my desire to capitalize and maximize our time together.

Arriving early for the next practice, I felt more jittery, as if I had to perfect the pieces we played previously. Asal once again welcomed me, and I noticed how her grey tunic dress blended into the grey walls with the minimalist furniture in a palette of black and white. There were few distractions here. The music stand was prepared in its place.

"Do you require additional light for your music?" she asked graciously. "Would you like some water?"

I organized myself in my seat, then adjusted the length of my cello and the tension on the bow.

"I'm good to go, thanks," I said, trying to conceal my apprehension about starting.

We immediately jumped into the Beethoven minuet we'd discussed. I began with an incorrect note, and my ears were ablaze with the faulty intonation, my fingers wobbling, aware of each and every misplaced finger that followed.

Intonation is the chronic nemesis of every string player. Except for the guitar with its evenly spaced frets, all other string instruments demand a fingerboard memory that seems to take a lifetime to master. The challenge for the beginner is to learn to hit the right note consistently, making the woodwinds, the brass instruments, and the piano a romp in the park for beginners to play.

With no warm-up and wavering confidence in my skills, I was completely discouraged by my performance.

"It's perfectly natural," Asal reassured me, reading my facial expressions. "This is all part of the learning process. You're now taken out of your comfort zone and forced into an entirely new situation. Novel sounds coming from the piano in addition to the different acoustics in this room can so easily throw you off. Here you're fully exposed."

I realized then that I wasn't in the comfort of my practice cocoon or the familiar presence of Dobrochna, knowing full well that sounds varied with the setting. Even at home, Simone's resonance changed in each room, depending on the carpeting or flooring, the amount of furniture, the temperature. However, I felt like a child being given reassurance in the face of a simple failure. I was embarrassed at the need for my fragile ego to be propped up.

"Listen, Mavis, I think it might help if we pick up the tempo a bit. This is a dance, an elegant dance, not too fast but something moving, since it's written *gracioso*."

We played once again, picking up the tempo with no time to catch my breath. However, with a hastier tempo than I was accustomed to, I immediately tripped over my fingers. Then we continued with *Humoresque* and *La Cinquantaine* from the previous session.

In every case, I rode on top of the strings without applying any weight, an evasion tactic I'd developed reflexively when trying to avoid the amplification of errors. In other words, I broke all the rules and scrupulously learned play patterns mastered over the past months. My gains seemed to evaporate in one afternoon of playing. Even my earlier repertoire, once challenging but recently more manageable and comfortable, had turned into a nightmare.

"I know this is good for me," I admitted to Asal as we wound down the practice.

"Of course, you may get surprised in a negative way by what or how you're playing. But just remember, it's all part of your journey, of making progress and advancing."

As I left the spartan condo in the neighbourhood where my mother had lived, I remembered the past five years of her life when, every Saturday, we spent the day together. And I recalled that day when I announced, "I'm going to take up the cello," as she lay propped in her bed, staring at me in disbelief.

"Cello? At your age?" she'd asked, eyes wide open.

Perhaps my mother had known something I didn't or had been onto something I was too pigheaded to admit. Now I was feeling destroyed by my inability to coordinate my playing with another musician.

The following session with Asal turned out much more successfully. I learned that practising with a goal of performing with or for someone forced a level of engagement that wasn't present in everyday practice. I discovered that by setting a performance goal, be it for Lawlor, another teacher, a friend, or even an imaginary audience, helped me take my playing to another level of success.

After a few sessions together, Dobrochna suggested I wait to expand my repertoire before scheduling another time with Asal.

In that fall of 2021, my cello lessons with Dobrochna moved from my backyard to a building on tree-lined Beverley Street where students scurried by, winding their way to classes on the nearby St. George university campus. The building houses the Polish Combatants' Association (Stowarzyszenie Polskich Kombatantów), or SPK, as it's known to its members, an international association formed in 1946 by demobilized Polish servicemen and women. Today, it also functions as a Polish cultural centre.

As I unpacked Simone, Dobrochna bounced in, apologizing for being late. "Traffic, you know. And Toronto construction. You taught me, Mavis, that there are two seasons in Toronto — winter and construction." She immediately took out her cello and arranged the furniture, then without skipping a beat, said, "Now let's begin with a scale."

With utmost concentration in my whole being, I played a slowly bowed D major scale four octaves up to thumb position.

"Very good, very good," Dobrochna said. "But this time I want you to pay attention to the transition in order to nail down even more the intonation. Like this ..." And she demonstrated on her cello with deftness and ease.

Scales — the building blocks of every practice. If technique could be mastered on scales in slow, smooth movements, then that agility and dexterity could be transferred to pieces, or so the wisdom went.

On the cello, to master an even, fluid sound on every note demanded attention to the way the bow slid across the stings, the exact placement of the left hand on the fingerboard, and an even transition between pulling the bow down and pushing it seamlessly back up so that the shift in direction could barely be heard.

From there, we moved to some technical études that included a warm-up for trills and vibrato proficiency, a willful summoning of the brain to perform finger calisthenics.

"Okay, now how about we start to work on a new piece?" Dobrochna suggested, flipping through my book. "How about we approach a Bach composition?"

It wasn't just any composition Dobrochna proposed that day, but a minuet for one of the famous cello suites written by the legendary composer and *sine qua non* of every cello player. I'd listened to the suites played by Yo-Yo Ma, Mischa Maisky, Stephen Isserlis, Daniel Shafran, and others, read their well-documented history in Eric Siblin's informative book, *The Cello Suites*,[1] and knew their weightiness within the cello repertoire, the seriousness with which each generation of cellists aspired to match performances against the titans of the profession.

"You know I'm not a fan of the Baroque or the Bach suites," I confessed sheepishly, as if uttering a heretical statement. "A bit too mathematical, too cerebral for me. They just don't grab me."

Dobrochna laughed. I'm sure you'll change your mind one day. Wait and see."

Feeling chastised like a child, I shook my head in irritation. How many times had my mother condescendingly told me, "Just wait and see. When you get older, you'll change your mind."

In the meantime, under the low lighting of the room and the watchful eye of Andrzej Tadeusz Bonawentura Kościuszko, the Polish statesman and general staring out at a field of fallen soldiers in the painting on the wall in front of me, I focused my eyes on the music notes: my first step in learning Minuets I and II from Bach's Suite No. 1 in G Major, BWV 1007 from my *Suzuki Book 4*, a milestone in my cello journey! Of course, after spending time in Bach's company, I, too, discovered some of the glorious mystery hidden in the suites.

The first eve of Rosh Hashanah, the Jewish New Year, the first of the Days of Awe, is a sacred time of contemplation, reflection, and repentance. After the Covid shutdown for indoor activities, I decided to host the first evening meal, a tradition I'd maintained for many years. In addition to friends and family, I invited Dobrochna. She asked if she could bring her cello, saying, "I'd like to surprise your friends with some playing." Then she added, "And what about you? Would you like to play a duet with me for your people?"

I knew I'd be super-busy with cooking and meal preparation, but I agreed, anyway. We chose two short pieces for me to play: the Kummer étude for two cellos that had moved Lawlor so much in the summer and another solo Bach piece.

One day before the celebration, I fell apart under the pressure and decided it was too much to handle. I planned to wait until the next day to inform Dobrochna, but during my morning practice, I was much improved and played surprisingly smoothly. So, I changed my mind and resolved to go for it.

When the guests arrived and all the arrangements for the meal were in place, I brought my cello downstairs to set up with Dobrochna off the kitchen. I was off to a poor start on the first piece and told Dobrochna the tempo was too slow. We began the duet again, my fingers fumbling, anticipating my nervousness, but I persisted and played through. Dobrochna's steady, passionate performance helped me along, and then I was on my own for the solo Bach. For once, I was pleased with my playing.

Relaxed after my effort, I was mesmerized by Dobrochna's playing of pieces I was very familiar with: the beautiful *Prayer From the Jewish Suite, No. 1* by Ernest Bloch; the Prelude from Bach's Suite No. 1; and the Sarabande from his Suite No. 3.

"Do you realize you lift your toes when you're playing a scale?" Dobrochna asked after our Rosh Hashanah performance. "I think you need to find some beanbags to weight your feet."

I ordered a set of throw-and-toss beanbags for children, but they were too light and small to be of any assistance. Margot from the Pilates studio suggested five-pound bags of rice. Then I remembered Lawlor's ankle weights, which worked like a charm.

"Look at me," I said to Dobrochna at my next lesson, sloshing my feet in my new blue ankle weights.

"But your toes are still curling."

I can't believe this, I thought. *Always something else.*

I spoke to Margot again. "I have the perfect solution for you," she told me. "Toe separators."

I thought she was joking and burst out laughing. "You're kidding, right?"

"No, really, Mavis. This would be perfect for what you need." And, as if knowing I'd do anything to improve my cello performance, she added, "And we happen to have some at the studio. If you'd like, I can put aside a pair at the front desk and you can come by whenever it's convenient." The instructions on the box of toe separators read like an advertisement for New Age gear: "Zen format. Benefits include toe alignment and opening of the body's centre."

My collection of cello paraphernalia kept growing: ankle weights and toe separators, both tastefully matched in cobalt blue, to anchor my lower body, especially when practising vibrato; a spiky tennis ball, also in blue, to ensure my correct right-hand position; varietals of rosin, a form of tree resin, used on bow hairs to increase friction between the bow and strings; a soft cloth for cleaning my cello after each use; and the latest addition, a cello bow form placed across the strings that ensured proper position and technique. When I unwrapped my new acquisition exported from Ann Arbor, Michigan, it turned out also to be blue with white rubber panels on either side to attach to the inner bouts of the A and C strings. All these cello accoutrements lived in a small plastic basket, around which the cello stand, cello bench, cello mirror, and floor guard huddled like a chamber group.

Dobrochna laughed when I described the overflow. "That's what happens with the cello. It begins to take over."

And, of course, it was usually at her instigation that my musical collection multiplied.

Before Christmas, I stopped by Remenyi House of Music where large banners in the front window announced a closing-out sale with *big* discounts. I decided it was time to purchase a new stand. Almost from the beginning, Dobrochna had railed against my flimsy portable music stand capable of holding only one music book at a time and sliding recklessly with any slight movement.

The salesperson at Remenyi showed me three stands, and as in "Goldilocks and the Three Bears," I thought, "This one was too flimsy like mine, that one was too big and bulky like conservatory weight, and this one was just right, a solid stand that could still be reduced in size for transporting.

"Now in order to receive the seventy percent discount on the $40 stand," the salesperson said, "you'll unfortunately need to buy some additional goods. Do have a look around the store."

I ambled about the downstairs and added four books, also reduced, to my purchases: Oliver Sacks's *Musicophilia*; *The Music Instinct* by Philip Ball; Alex Ross's *Listen to This*, a classic collection of essays written for *The New Yorker*; and *Words Without Music*, a memoir by Philip Glass, one of my favourite contemporary composers. But I was still short for the discount.[2]

I left the store weighed down with my music stand in its black nylon carrying case; four books; two pairs of socks, one set black-embossed with musical notes and another orange with black piano keys; a treble clef–shaped eraser; and a notepad with the design of a violin on its cover. More props for my cello collection.

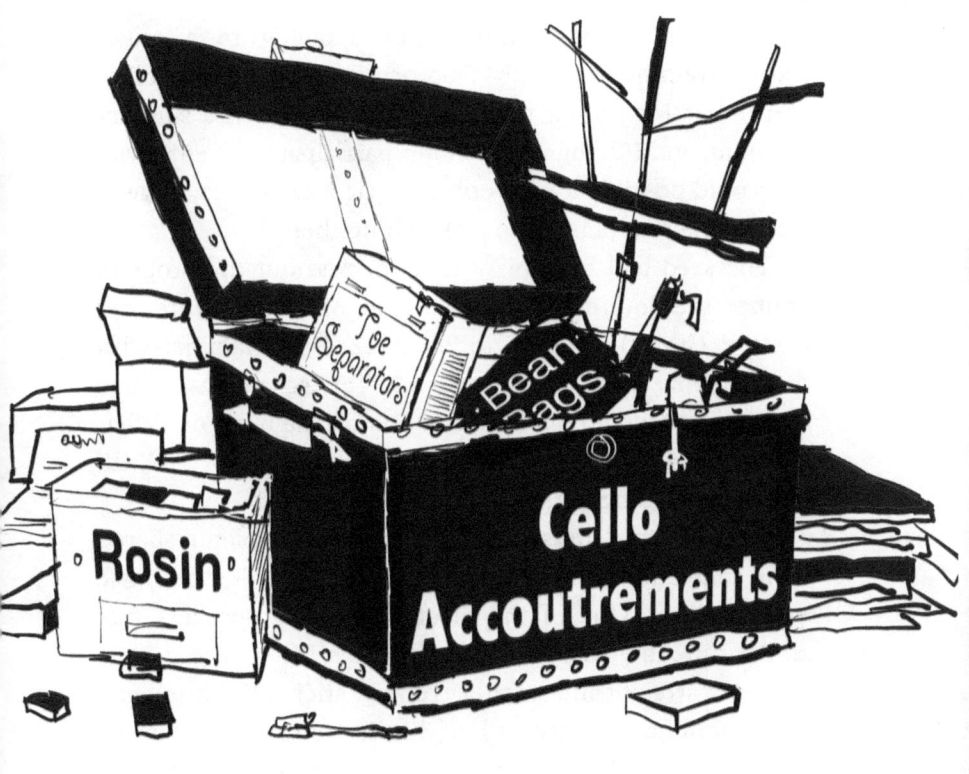

16

Learning Cello Online

"What do you think about applying to a music festival training program?" Dobrochna asked, always full of surprises. "My former teacher in Baltimore runs a summer program, and I thought you might participate. Given Covid, you could possibly attend online. That way, you could get a feel for the program without travelling there."

The seed had been planted. I checked out the program online: the Intermuse International Music Institute and Festival (IIMIF), June 16 to 25, 2022. I was familiar with the name because Dobrochna had invited me two years earlier to attend an online workshop on the topic of "What Is Music? How to Do Music," given by a number of IIMIF alumni, including herself.

For an hour, musicians of strings and piano shared their convictions and notions about the meaning of music in their lives. One of the most captivating speakers was an African American who described his life with music as hitting a straight line with a crooked stick. Disadvantaged as an immigrant, stripped of his language and identity, he represented his life journey as an exploration in self-expression. Referring to his musical outlet as a survival tactic, he highlighted his belief that at the core of his culture was a resilience evidenced in the heritage of blues, spirituals, hip-hop, rap, and classical. He spoke compellingly about the fundamental humanity of music that forever transcended boundaries and borders. This elegant-looking gentleman with his Afro and traditional robe reinforced for me the motto proposed by IIMIF: "Inhale Life, Exhale Music."

"Are you kidding me?" I asked Dobrochna after googling the entry requirements and application process. "Performances, concerts, repertoire, *plus* a tape of your playing." This was so way beyond my comfort zone; I had no idea how to complete the application form. Yet the thought of a ten-day intense program with three private classes, three master classes, lectures and workshops, and evening concerts appealed to me.

Summer music festivals and camps mushroom every summer around the globe. From the narrow streets of the Cremona International Music Academy and Festival in Italy to the Killington Music Festival in Vermont's Green Mountains, from the Carl Flesch Akademie held in a cultural landmark in the spa town of Baden-Baden, Germany, to Le Festival International du Domaine Forget in the hamlet of Saint-Irénée, Charlevoix, Quebec, students of all ages flock to academies and institutes to create a community and share music. Interestingly, most programs stipulate age ranges, some limiting the upper cutoff at sixty or sixty-five.

Incensed at what appeared to be clear ageism, I wondered how I might be perceived by a young group of musicians. Would they not want to include me in a small group or choose me last? Would they be willing to share a music stand with someone old enough to be their mother or even grandmother?

I knew Dobrochna had written her teacher, Cecylia Barczyk, to find out if the IIMIF would be willing to accept a student at my level and age. She called me a few nights later. "They accept people at all levels of playing. You know, I feel it's very important for musicians to work with students of all levels and to mix together."

"Easy for you to say. I'm just not sure how I'll mingle with all these young adults. Maybe they'll feel I'm too … I don't know what … old?"

"Listen," Dobrochna said calmly, "Cecylia was one of my teachers. I know her children, all musicians, who run the program. Let me help you go through the application if you're really interested. Forget about your self-consciousness and age, but don't forget to showcase what you wish to work on while there."

Eventually, I answered all the questions and made an audiotape of my playing with Asal on piano — two duets from my *Suzuki Book 3*, plus one of the solo Bach minuets — then filed the application and paid the fee. Asked if I wished to participate in a master class, I answered "undecided"; queried about performing in the closing student concert, I replied "undecided." As it turned out, I did neither.

My first attempt at sending out the material was unsuccessful, so I called the registrar for technical assistance. Apparently, I was applying to the Interharmony, not Intermuse, International Music Festival, another online event in Boca Raton, Florida. A true Freudian slip no analyst could miss! Once that was sorted out, I succeeded in transmitting all my material before the deadline.

Then I forgot about the program until six weeks later when I received an email with my acceptance. I was convinced Dobrochna had put in a good word for me with the powers that be, likely stressing my life experience as well as my commitment and dedication to my instrument.

At the introductory session on the first day, I learned that twenty-five people had been admitted into the program, twenty-two in person and three of us online. As each of the cherub-like youngsters introduced their names, their objectives, and a brief statement of their musical histories, I realized that among this cohort were two dozen students ranging in age from sixteen to twenty-two, *plus* me. Oh, and one of our number was an eleven-year-old piano child prodigy.

I chuckled with Lawlor after that first meeting online. "A bunch of babes. Maybe I should consider turning off my video next time so I can remain incognito and no one can see the senior citizen of the group."

Over the next ten days, I stopped my professional practice and immersed myself in the musical experience, or as much as I could online. As a remote learner, I was unable to participate in the small group ensemble classes, and due to the back surgery I'd had as an adolescent, I couldn't participate in the midday yoga program with its high demand on full-body extensions.

A class schedule was circulated every evening, and students were encouraged to attend all events. I sat in on the master classes for violins, cellos, and pianos; attended workshops on alchemy in the practice room, on conducting and singing, on instrument care and selection, and onstage presence; witnessed evening concerts performed by faculty and guest performers; and enjoyed three private classes on Zoom with Cecylia Barczyk, a highlight of the program. Despite my initial nervousness, Cecylia's sensitivity to my age and musical progression gave me the confidence to relax during our lessons.

With Cecylia, I practised *vibrato* as if I were moving salt shakers up and down the strings, using quarter notes at first, starting with my fourth finger, then my third before attempting the others. I learned to put more weight in my left hand with intention and to tap on the string to develop stronger resonance. She taught me to anticipate the music and to hear it before playing, tips I'd also been given by Dobrochna, only expressed in a different manner.

When I felt my "baby pieces" didn't warrant being taken seriously, Cecylia dismissed this as an excuse to avoid placing myself more inside the music. My greatest takeaway from her approach was a newfound engagement of expression. At the same time, being of the same generation, we found common ground and shared the pleasures of triumph in later-life learning. Cecylia admitted that after a recent move to the countryside in Ohio, she'd found a new love of gardening.

Next to the private sessions, the other highlight was the evening check-in where we all gathered at the end of the day to share comments, insights, obstacles, and successes. The group already knew me as the woman who picked up the cello at the age of most of their grandmothers. They were used to my online presence in the group sessions and heard me express my desire to be as fully included in the program as those involved in person.

One night I shared an article I'd read that day in *The Strad* about an illustrious but little-known French composer of the late eighteenth century. This man had insisted technique should always be in the service of expression and that one needed not only to play with one's fingers but with one's soul. That suggestion had echoed a comment made earlier in the day by a faculty member who reminded us to "bring all of your heart and conviction to your playing."

In our individual exit interviews with a faculty member, I shared my concerns about remote involvement and my inability to completely partake in certain aspects of the program. While I admired the sense of camaraderie I saw develop among the participants, I also wondered if my actual physical presence would have disturbed the dynamics, given my outlier status in age.

"Oh, Mavis," the faculty member assured me, "I can't tell you how much everyone enjoyed your participation. They seemed to gravitate to you and always remembered to jot down anything you may have missed in a program. And when you spoke, they all quieted down to hear what you had to say. It was our pleasure to have you participate and clearly theirs, as well."

I blushed over the Skype call. Who was to know that at the end of the ten days I'd be named "Queen of IIMIF 2022" by a group of students who created mock certificates for each participant and that less than six months later I'd be offering a workshop to their alumni entitled "Portrait of the Musician as an Artist: Musings from an Aspiring Cellist"?

17

Exploring Simone's Roots

Standing in an old-growth forest of white and red pines in Temagami in northeastern Ontario, I was seized by a feeling of solemnity and silence, respect and awe. Lawlor walked up to one of the immense trees facing us and stretched his arms to embrace it. Encircling the gnarled trunk for a moment, he broke the quietude. "Mavis, come here and feel the energy. Come and listen to its wisdom. It's all here, all in here. Just try to imagine what this tree has experienced."

My husband with the Zen Buddhist soul once again reminded me of the power of trees, the life-giving and life-sustaining force of these majestic conifers. I followed his instructions, hugged another tree, and felt my heart pound against its bark, unable to fathom the life history of this grand pine.

Suzanne Simard, in *Finding the Mother Tree: Discovering the Wisdom of the Forest*, writes in her inspiring and well-documented book: "The trees soon revealed startling secrets." She discovers an arboreal "web of interdependence" among the forest growth that produces a silent transmission of "intimacy and wisdom." This British Columbia ecologist concludes that diversity matters and that "everything in the universe *is* connected — between the forests and prairies, the land and the water, the sky and the soil, the spirits and the living, the people and all other creatures."[1]

I pictured the performance of an orchestral ensemble of trees, communicating non-verbally through a network of gestures and postures, branches bending, roots reaching, leaves lilting, a shared cadence of communication, a silent symphony. Throughout centuries of oral transmission, elders have taught us the sentient world extends beyond the confinement of the strictly human sphere. Within their cosmology, sensed, sensorial, sense-ible, and sensuous phenomena are all as alive and aware as we humans.

Simard's book was the most recent one I'd read highlighting the mutual interdependence between man and nature. The ecologist and anthropologist David Abram similarly discusses the way the sentient world and each organism are intertwined, writing: "There is a subtle entanglement and confusion between all beings of the earth, a consequence not only of our common ancestry, and the cellular similarities of our makeup, but also of our subjection to variant aspects of the whirling world."[2] Infused by his animistic leanings, Abram's book sensually describes the powerful bonds between humans and animals and the blurred boundaries between mind and earth. Also unfettered by symbols and sentences, he claims the tension expressed by sound and movement aren't "entirely incommensurable."

We know trees contain within themselves not only the story of their lifelines but also the historical mapping of our cultural history. Arboreal gifts bestowed upon us from trees include bows and arrows; pine rocking cradles and poplar coffins; chewing gum, sponges, and wine corks; hardwood floors and baseball bats; papers and books; and pianos, violins, and cellos.

Simard ends her book with a sobering conclusion. She reminds us both of our need for trees and our obligation to give back to them. That we're now more aware of the intelligence and spiritual quality of trees akin to that of our species places an onus of responsibility critical to our decision-making. Accordingly, we must consider "a philosophy of treating these world's creatures, its gifts, as of equal importance to us. This begins by recognizing that trees and plants have agency."[3]

I thought about my cello and my bow. What were Simone's origins? From what tree did my pernambuco bow come? Had I contributed to nature's destruction in the purchase of my beloved Simone? On the other hand, if trees are the lungs of the earth, as scientists say, then am I not playing trees and allowing them to perform?

At the conclusion of one cello lesson, I spoke to Dobrochna about my recent reading, as well as my cello journey and the hope of one day detailing it.

Carefully dressing her cello in its floral silk dressing gown, Dobrochna stopped mid-action and gazed up at me. "If you really want to understand the cello and your own cello experience, I suggest you go back to the beginning, to the cello itself. And if you really want to understand the relationship between a cellist and her instrument, then you must look at the actual birth of the cello. You could always interview some luthiers, those people who transform wood into instruments, fashioning them to come alive with music. If you like, I can suggest some names to you."

Dobrochna continued to tell me about these talented artisans. "Instrument makers are very different. Some have a very spiritual side and others don't. I'd say there are even differences between male and female luthiers, with their own unique sensitivities and proclivities incorporated into their work. After all, wood is organic and living. It responds to a person's touch."

I smiled. Perhaps she'd read the same books on the wisdom of trees as I had.

One winter day, I found myself at the front door of a house with four large evergreens draped in snow in Toronto's Upper Beach. Walking down the shovelled path, sparkling snow crystals dancing in the sunlight, I recalled brilliant days in Montreal when the city streets turned into a wonderland of white-cloaked princesses on parade. I knocked on the door and was ushered inside by a slight woman with a generous smile and raven hair in a ponytail.

"Come in, come in," Itzel Ávila said with a Spanish accent. "Did you have a problem finding this place? I hope my instructions were clear."

An invitation for coffee was followed up with an espresso, a jug of water, and a plate of biscotti, all delicately served on a violin-shaped tray. As we sat on the sofa, I noticed an upright piano of shiny wood with a protective red runner covering the keyboard like a handwoven amulet.

Two paintings hung over the piano. In the foreground of one, a woman in a red-and-white dress with an elaborate mane of black hair rode a black bicycle, while in the background a green forest of trees hid a cityscape in blue. A sun hovered in the sky like a suspended ball in the blue-grey clouds. In the second, a man was upside down in a black suit with one hand on the bike seat, his other hand pointed at the handlebars. A red bird sat perched on the green frame of the bike. The forest was gone, but the cityscape remained and the moon still levitated in the sky.

As we sat and drank coffee, Itzel shared some insights about her craft. Forgetting to bring a tape recorder, I asked, "Is it okay if I take notes?"

"Certainly." Then she began. "I'm at the service of the wood. The wood has its own path. I respect it and trust it'll lead and direct me." She paused, seemingly lost in thought, then continued. "The wood owns me, and I'm merely the medium listening to it. The wood is the blank page of the writer, the ball of the artist's clay. I'm like the sculptress who creates curves. I believe wood is feminine, and I'll make of her the most beautiful instrument. So ... what debt do I have to this wood that'll become the voice for someone else?"

"How did you get started making musical instruments?" I asked, sipping my espresso and taking a bite of biscotti.

"I made violins and cellos from a young age. Growing up in a household surrounded by music, the keyboard was my initiation into the world of music. I was the youngest of four children and my parents ran out of energy and encouragement to support my talents, so I was unable to pursue my keyboard interests."

"How old were you when you discovered the violin?" I prompted.

"I was a teenager," she replied. "I wanted to play music, so I went to the conservatory, but they didn't have any pianos. Instead, I was given a violin, which ultimately changed everything. The only available option was a Chinese violin, commercially made and very basic. At fifteen, I had no money to invest in a proper instrument. In China at that time, everything was mass-produced, and more significantly, it was all at the hands of child labour. You make this with that, you use these different woods and those different varnishes. Today, those children have been replaced by machines doing the same task of slapping wood together on assembly lines. So, I decided to visit a violin maker in town and requested he make a violin. My family couldn't afford to buy one."

She looked at me with her captivating smile. "That was the opening into another universe for me. I began apprenticing with this man and couldn't give up making or playing music. I was so, so ... no ... I am so very stubborn." Laughing, she picked up a violin just completed and began to play. "It was a gift, I was to learn, something very precious placed into my hands — my work with the magical mystery of wood."

She finished playing and put the violin gently down on her worktable. "It needs more tuning. Words aren't my language, not my *natural* language. I'd say music is my language and making instruments my way of giving voice to that musical expression."

Itzel's studio work was in an alcove off the living room with maximum sunlight created by the bay windows. On her desk, a small gooseneck lamp provided additional illumination. Surrounded on all sides by shelves showcasing an assortment of miniature tools, Itzel moved with a minimum of motion among wood scraps, cans of neck-graft rabbit glue, and jam jars filled with varnish. One wall was lined with a corkboard of clamps, chisels, scrapers, and calipers, along with an assortment of fine-pointed brushes and *schmattes*. These accoutrements were the paraphernalia with which Itzel rasped and sanded, joined and sliced, sweated and laboured.

Eight violins hung from a rack on the side wall with four above the front window. On another wall were two bunches of bow hair, one straw-coloured, the other black, both longer than the four bows they were perched beside. Wooden frames and templates lay on their sides under the worktable, while boxes were filled with pieces of wood and tools. Itzel was a master craftswoman and the current president of the Makers' Forum, the Canadian association of professional creators of violins and bows.

"I've never actually held a violin in my hands," I admitted to Itzel.

She immediately placed the one she'd just played into my hands. A violin weighs less than half a kilogram — the weight of three medium-sized apples, three large chicken drumsticks, or twice the weight of a hamster but one-fifth of a chihuahua. By contrast, the average cello weighs around three kilograms — the weight of a large bag of oranges, four sizable textbooks, or a big sack of rice.

"This lightweight instrument becomes an extension of your arm when playing," she told me. "It's like we're playing trees in some way. We make trees sing."

"Could you explain the process of making a cello to me?" I asked.

"The instrument maker begins with a dead piece of wood. Think about that — a dead piece of wood transformed into a very alive, uplifting, and soul-moving sound. The cello, the violin, the viola all sing for us, and their sound touches hearts, lighting up a part of us like universal stars."

Itzel explained the complex process of choosing the wood. Having apprenticed as a luthier in Italy, she was familiar with Italian woods, which led her to the woodlands of southern Europe. "I'm a snob when it comes to wood. I'm partisan and simply try to find the woods that speak to me. I've returned from my search expeditions with back pieces from Switzerland and top pieces from New Brunswick in eastern Canada. Imagine that! Wood is chosen by its density. The denser the wood, the better the quality. I must admit, though, my reluctance to use Canadian woods because of their particular dryness, making them more susceptible to cracking over time."

In the glow of her tiny workshop, I learned how woods varied in shades of colour but also created tones of colour. For example, the tanning of sunlight through increased exposure bronzed the wood. An instrument of deep amber might contain many resins that went into the varnish. Different varnishes actually resulted in different tones and shades of music production. The age of the tree was determined by counting the rings in the wood: the dark representing winter, the light signifying summer. Consequently, one could read climate changes over the years by examining the patterns of these rings.

"Here, let me show you," Itzel said, disappearing, then returning with two slabs of wood and setting one on top of her shoe. "Traditionally, two pieces of matching spruce or pine, like this, make up the top of the instrument and help project the sound. Two f-holes carved on each side create the openings through which the sound is produced. The f-holes are the mouths from which the cello sings. Two pieces of matching maple are chosen for the back as well as the ribs, neck, and scroll, the last being the ornamental finish of the string instruments. Ebony, a hardwood that can support the playing, is then used for the fingerboard.

"So some of what you do is for aesthetic reasons, right?" I ventured.

Itzel smiled. "Yes, while there's limited freedom in the structure of the instrument, the woods lend aesthetic variation. And for the makers of instruments, colour adds an even further dimension of originality." Itzel laughed. "I sometimes put blue on certain spots of my instruments. It's a freedom in design like my own personal signature." Becoming serious again, she added, "Colour's like texture the eye can see. The projection of sound is like the light in the picture. Sound has no words ... like wine. But sound does have the scent of an *eau de parfum*. It leaves a trace."

Once again, Itzel picked up the violin she was working on and began playing. "Not quite it. I want more on the G string. I may need to take it apart to fix it." In working attire — long apron, jeans, and boots — she faced the window for a few minutes. "Here, Mavis, come and see this." First, she lowered a light and an *azul*, a tiny instrument the size of a dentist's pliers, inside the opening of the f-hole. "The sound post is the most important part of any string instrument, be it violin, viola, cello, or bass. In Spanish, we call it the *alma*, the soul of the instrument, like the French *âme*."

I glanced at the sound post, a tiny cylindrical piece of wood that resembled a three-inch straw or cigarette.

"The sound post has to be in a precise position, since it delicately connects the back and front of the instrument, supporting the pressure of the strings through the bridge. All sound reacts because all vibrations are connected. The sound post must be perfectly parallel with the base bar. If you move it slightly from the bridge to the base, it'll respond in different ways. For example, if tight, it'll have a brilliant, tight sound, but if it's more relaxed, the sound will be less brilliant."

I watched Itzel jiggle the matchstick piece of wood with intricate care. After a few minutes of intense focus and concentration, she stood, straightened, and began to play the violin. To my ear, the sound was lovely, but Itzel announced her displeasure. After several failed attempts, she tried one more time. My muscles had become tense from my site of observation behind her.

With the gentleness of a jewellery maker, the skill of a neurosurgeon, and the patience of a modeller, Itzel once again peered into the peephole, reinserted the *azul*, and realigned the sound post, determining the fate of the instrument's musicality.

When I was about to leave, I came face to face with a wall of bookshelves lined with foreign-titled books: Spanish, French, Italian, plus a small ink drawing elegantly positioned in front of a volume by the Colombian writer Fernando Vallejo. The sketch was entitled *Burrito II*, with a mule elegantly attired in a black shirt, pants, and bowtie riding a bicycle.

"My husband's a cyclist," she said, noticing my gaze. "As you can see, we have a collection of artworks to show off his hobby. Itzel and her husband, a professor of Spanish literature at York University, had both moved from Mexico to Toronto twenty years ago.

When I reappeared at the Heinl store a few months later to interview Ric Heinl, I was greeted by Noreen, the calm and friendly receptionist who gestured for me to have a seat in the familiar wing-backed chair with the cello endpin strap attached to its leg.

"Hey, you," Ric said in a greeting that hinted at a certain familiarity we had now. This time I recognized the bushy hair, a reminder of Covid's impact on our grooming habits, the serene smile, and reflective eyes. Once again uniformed in his blue apron and working pants, white shirt with sleeves rolled up, and striped tie, he seemed like a hybrid of a tradesman and executive. "Let's meet upstairs where the coffee supplies live," he said.

We soon settled at a round table surrounded by bottles of extra virgin olive oil, spring onion crackers, chocolates, breadsticks, shortbread cookies, and jars of sour cherry jam and manuka honey. Pre-Christmas festivities had clearly arrived in this kitchen on the second floor. Sipping coffee, we began discussing the family business he'd expanded, the musical children he'd adopted, the parents of students he'd reassured and supported, and the celebrities and virtuosos he'd entertained.

Despite the informality of his demeanour, Ric was a rare person with an extraordinary sensitivity to his craft. His workmanship and knowledge have garnered his shop a positive reputation among the most sophisticated instrument houses in Europe. He is a raconteur, and it didn't take much to launch him into his storytelling.

"One day, a young student, maybe twenty-two or twenty-three, came to the shop wishing to upgrade his instrument. He owned a 1920 Scarampella violin,[4] a pure instrument with no cracks or defects. Pure perfection. I told him he was growing and developing with a highly desired violin he should explore and cherish. I insisted he keep it rather than exchange his instrument. Then I wished him the best of luck. Six days later, I received a phone call from the young man's father, heartbroken and weeping. 'My son,' he sobbed, 'slipped and fell in the ice storm we had here in Vancouver and landed on his instrument.' And so there followed a very lengthy and ongoing process of restoration of this extremely valuable instrument. One hundred years after its birth, the instrument almost died. So, you see, nothing's permanent. Owning an instrument is only a temporary guardianship."

I eyed the last biscotti on the plate.

Ric grinned. "Go for it, Mavis." Then he continued. "Another time, a husband and wife came into my store with a violin that had been in the family for many years. Not sure of its value but before offering it up to a garage sale, they decided to do due diligence and took it to Long & McQuade to assess its value. The staff there suggested bringing it to me. Turns out they were the owners of a $250,000 Vuillaume violin that the family then had restored and gave to the Canada Council."

Ric is a talented psychologist attuned to subtle nuances in people. "From the first encounter, I see how a person moves, how they look. I read their body language and the way they handle an instrument. Whether I'm repairing an instrument or introducing a new one for purchase, I have to get a sense of the person. For example, if people come in to see me about sound post adjustments, I watch them play, noting where they push, where they pull, et cetera. Then I can create a space for that instrument to sing. That's when the magic begins.

"Everything has energy, natural energy. An instrument's full of energy. It's waiting to share its energy with you. The wood talks to me. It talks to me when I touch it. Each individual piece of wood has its own energy. To produce a violin or cello with these particular pieces of energy is to create a work of art. You can't impose yourself on the object. You have to work with its own spirit."

"Is there some role you particularly see yourself as doing?" I asked when I got the chance.

"Yes, there is. I facilitate relationships between the artist and his or her instrument. I wouldn't call myself a matchmaker exactly, because the relationships I help forge aren't for life. The musician is the custodian of the instrument, a temporary one, never a full-time owner. Sure, I bring instruments together with people and vice versa, but it's a union between two forces of energy in the end. The energy of the instrument and the energy of the person both do their own dances. The less I push, the more they work things out between them."

Coffee finished and the biscotti eaten, we adjourned for the day so Ric could get back to work. When we met again a few days later, we were in his office on the third floor of Heinl's. Like my mother had been, Ric was also an aesthete. Not only did he cherish elegant instruments but also fine jewellery, antique books, and precious *objets d'art*, including a sketch of Pablo Casals behind his desk, a clothesline of bows hanging on one wall, multiple violins and violas suspended from the ceiling, and cellos and basses standing like soldiers in orchestral formation.

So mesmerized by the artwork and bric-a-brac in this museum of musical delights, I said, "I'd love to spend an afternoon exploring your treasures."

Ric flashed a smile. "Come here and I'll show you something." He indicated a framed opening where there was a crawl space on the side of the wall. Inside, I saw scores of miniature violins, doll-sized, like a child's garden of playthings. "My private stock," he said proudly. "I've always loved these tiny pieces."

I figured Ric likely knew something about dendrochronology, the technique of dating instruments by studying their ring patterns. It was a subject Itzel had brought up when I interviewed her. "We humans try so hard to hide our age with lotions, potions, and creams, while trees reveal their ages so unabashedly and without any concealment."

Ric chuckled at my observation. "Instruments also have personal memories. When a good musician plays an instrument, the vibrations of the strings running through its body massage the wood and teach the cells how to move together. The way a violin vibrates is the key to its sound, and since it never forgets what it's learned, it'll continue to carry the imprint of former players in its voice and perhaps even a memory of the music, as well."

"I read somewhere," I said, "that instruments can be so deeply inscribed with the legacies of extraordinary musicians that a violinist trying one for the first time often says the instrument seems to will her or him to play it in a certain way, as if it wants to slip back into routines and practices of a former owner."

Ric nodded. "Exactly! Each instrument has its own personality. Musicians often speak of their instruments' quirks and idiosyncrasies, shortcomings and limitations, capriciousness and fickleness, prowess and pluckiness. Furthermore, each instrument forms a bond with its owner such that if you were to borrow an instrument of a virtuoso for a few days, even hours, the musician would know someone else had been playing it. In other words, your contact with an instrument leaves an impression or has an impact on its intonation and sound, enough to be detected by its owner. But here's what I find most interesting. Not only would the owner notice someone played his or her instrument, but he or she would also learn something from that experience. Imagine! Of course, you have to understand we're talking about instruments like the Strads or Amatis known for their consistency and excellence."

Excitedly, he continued. "Here's another situation. If I were to give Dobrochna a Strad cello and leave her in a studio for an hour, she'd likely say, 'I always heard Strads were hard to play, but after an hour, I knew what it wanted from me and then it wasn't so hard.' You see, the Strad isn't forgiving, but in the hands of great artists who can get into its groove, it can give them the world."

"And what if I were to play one?" I asked hesitantly. "What would happen then?"

"Well, it would still perform for you, but perhaps without the *wow* factor it would for your teacher."

"So, Ric what can you tell me about Simone?

"I purchased your cello from a dealer and friend named Howard Morgan who has a violin shop in Wales. In the velvet-curtained rooms at the Park Plaza Hotel in Toronto, 400 or so dealers come to buy and swap, comparing notes and prices, but still keeping cards close to their chests. We're each our own hunters and gatherers. Dealers come with their special stock and items on the lookout for corporate business. We all buy something and hope it carries the authentic label with no broken sound post or purling damage.

"As for your dear instrument, I happened to see this petite seven-eighths cello there and was immediately attracted to her," he continued, as if speaking about a woman he'd just met. "I'm a sucker for small bows and violins, so not surprisingly, I was drawn to your Simone. I spoke to Howard and was told Simone was commissioned by someone wanting a smaller piece. I don't know who that owner was, but I'll find out for you so you'll have Simone's complete history."

Later, I learned that Howard no longer remembered the source of Simone's origins, due to cognitive decline.

I was introduced to Michèle Ashley and her unconventional history through a Zoom encounter. Dividing her time between Montreal and Boston, Michèle began her career as a budding cellist. However, a chance event altered the course of her life. Having observed a craftsman once repair her damaged cello on a flight, she became so fascinated by his work that she changed career paths. She applied to an instrument-making school in Cremona, Italy, and was accepted into a program. Shocked that Michèle was a female in a male-dominated field, the school sent her to a convent for her residence. Her teacher told her it was a waste of time to study and that she should get married and have babies.

At that time, in the 1970s, Michèle had a hard time being a young woman in Italy. Her free time was spent warding off men who tried hitting on her. Fortunately, she befriended a British woman who happened to be studying in the same field.

Her class of contemporaries was a cohort of young Italian boys offered the vocational options of woodworking or making music. Having already satisfied some of the requirements, Michèle was able to advance in the program. While studying, she apprenticed for three years in a shop where she met her first husband. They were both subsequently hired by the same violin maker who bought them a semi-finished house in a remote village near Parma in the Apennines. They repaid for the house by making violins and restoring instruments.

Villagers gawked at the foreign couple who had invaded their prosciutto-making hamlet. I visualized the house Michèle described where a bread oven in the basement below the kitchen heated the home and shop alongside cows.

The exotic intruders were soon welcomed by the community, which fed and protected them. The first television, purchased in the village ten years earlier, was donated to the couple because the villagers felt this was something Michèle and her husband could enjoy together. At one point, to supplement their earnings, Michèle worked in the fields with some of the local widowed women and was paid with cheese, ham, and bread.

After six years of struggling and suffering to make ends meet, they moved with their daughter to Verona and set up a shop. The marriage fell apart, and each of them set up their own independent shops, mainly making violins and violas. When her ex-husband hurt his hand, preventing him for any further work in the field, Michèle continued to produce and restore instruments.

In 1985, after fifteen years of living in Italy, Michèle and her daughter moved to Boston where her sisters lived and set up her own shop. Her second husband is a producer and director for the French CBC and a professor at the University of Quebec in Montreal, while Michèle divides her time between Montreal and Boston. Due to the demands of making instruments and the toll it took on her hands, Michèle was forced to discontinue her music performances.

Unlike Ric, Michèle sees herself exactly as a matchmaker. "Instruments are the voices of musician, their companion. They'll spend more time with their cellos than with their partners. I'm very invested in this process, since it forms the most intimate of relationships. It's like a child between us, a creative partnership. I've created it and they'll express themselves through it. You see, it's a collaborative union."

Michèle described to me the idiosyncrasies noted in her clients. "Sometimes, before the concert, a musician will call and say, 'My cello isn't sounding like it used to,' and I'll suggest coming over for an adjustment. For some, I may not do anything to the instrument, but they walk away satisfied. In my work, I have a mental profile of my musicians. One violinist I knew had two fiddles and was in my shop every two weeks with a complaint. I knew he was lonely and just needed to chat and play. Another violist I worked with similarly came under the guise of some need, yet also just wanted comfort and reassurance."

With her instruments played by several internationally renowned musicians, Michèle emphasized the relationship and fit between instrument and musician, no matter what level of mastery. "It must be a good fit — the tone, the sound, the body of the instrument. It has to be right, and I try to consider and incorporate all the significant features and details I've been given before I create a commissioned instrument."

"What about old instruments versus newer ones?" I asked. "The older the better, no?"

"Not necessarily. Blind studies with both musicians and non-musicians alike aren't conclusive regarding the identity of old versus new instruments. There are an awful lot of fine instruments being made today that compare favourably with some treasures of the past. No consistency exists with all instruments born in Cremona, Verona, or wherever. We do know that wood plays a significant role in sound production. I've spent all my money and all my life fixing woods. At one point, I bought thirty years' worth of spruce from northern Italy and maple from the Baltic states."

I was itching to ask Michèle something but had hesitated so far. Now I took the leap. "What do you think the impact is of making instruments from old-growth stands of trees?"

She hesitated for a moment, then said with a smile, "That's a topic for another day."

I said goodbye to a woman whose life has been devoted to music and the gratification brought about by the sound of bow hairs on strings housed by wooden instruments whose designs date back centuries. Not only does she bring jubilation and euphoria to musicians and audiences alike, but she also creates a tonic of healing and a solarium of light for herself.

18

Second House Concert

*I*n my dream, I'm much younger. My hair is jet-black, the colour of my youthful curls. I wear a black tunic over a long black skirt with slits on the sides and my red brogue boots with black laces. I'm hunched over Simone in a full embrace, stretching my fingers into the demanding seventh position. Joyous and energized, I sway to "Life," a powerful piece by Ludovico Einaudi, the Italian composer.

I'm rapt in my dream with the music, seated between other renowned cellists and violinists. Angèle Dubeau, conductor of the La Pietà orchestra, peers up at me over her red-rimmed glasses and smiles in support and acknowledgement. I'm about to lose focus but am brought back to my playing by her nod. The others join in as we end the musical pleasantries we've been exchanging. Applause erupts from the audience members who immediately jump to their feet. Streamers and confetti are thrown onstage, and within seconds, the floor is carpeted in psychedelic colours.

When I awoke, my heart still pounded from the excitement, my forehead slick with sweat from the exertion.

What would I not give to be a member of such a highly acclaimed and high-calibre all-female ensemble as La Pietá? Just the previous night, I'd watched a concert on television celebrating twenty-five years of this talented chamber group founded by Dubeau. The anniversary concert was entitled "Elle" — *elle* in the singular despite the thirteen women (*elles*) comprising the group. *Elle*. Singular. Forever unique and without equal.

Angèle, baton slicing through the air, plus each of the twelve seated women, were dressed in black with a touch of red — a red hairpiece, a red belt, a red cummerbund, red stockings, red nail polish, a red bracelet, and Angèle with her square fire-engine red-framed glasses. This Montreal-based group, founded in 1997, overturned convention by bringing together an all-women group playing period recordings, subsequently transforming themselves into an ensemble showcasing such contemporary composers as Philip Glass, John Adams, Max Richter, and Arvo Pärt.

I, too, wished one day to perform and share my gift of making music with others. I, too, wanted to play with others and enjoy the cumulative impact of multiple musicians.

At my next lesson, I shared my dream with Dobrochna. She laughed. "It's great to dream big, to have sizable goals for yourself and not be discouraged by overreaching."

While the first two years of the Covid pandemic ravaged the world, putting an end to the luxury of indoor concerts, video streaming became the replacement for artists attempting to keep their professional interests alive. During what appeared to be a waning curve with restrictions on social gatherings lifted, I suggested to Dobrochna that we host another concert. This time I proposed we hold it in my backyard, which would be safer for those still feeling uncomfortable about socializing in indoor spaces.

The summer date wasn't conducive for the cellist Dobrochna tried to invite. Instead, she asked a violist, Caitlin Boyle, and we settled on a program for viola-cello duets. Dobrochna explained there was little repertoire composed for this pairing, but she'd include some pieces arranged specifically for both instruments. "We'll once again educate your friends and give them a panoramic view of music over time, including some twentieth-century pieces."

"As long as they're not too inaccessible or challenging," I said, knowing my friends' musical tastes regarding atonal, minimalist, or serial music.

Dobrochna placed her long fingers on her cello, sliding them up and down in a provocative manner. "You mean like this?" She laughed.

So, in the same fashion as our previous house concert, we underwent the process of planning, renting, and shopping. This time Dobrochna suggested I play a duet with her from my book for two cellos, followed by a couple of simple folk tunes (from *Singing Cellos*), duets we'd practised by Romuald Twardowski, a living Polish composer. I decided I could hide behind the anonymity of these pieces, since likely no one would have ever heard of Twardowski, now age ninety-two and once a student of Nadia Boulanger, the renowned and demanding pedagogue. And I began practising as much as I could, with Dobrochna reviewing and finalizing the program with me.

The morning before the scheduled concert, Dobrochna notified me she was ill and we'd have to postpone the concert — a typical pandemic parable and a lesson in resilience and adaptability. Covid had taught us how to make rapid programming changes, how to accommodate at the last moment, and how to find substitutions.

The rental chairs were already stacked on my front porch, the catered food waited to be picked up in the morning, and the wine was chilling in the refrigerator. I decided to salvage the event by asking friends to drop by for an afternoon of conversation and laughter. No music, no need to put on one's tennis gear, just food and fun.

We picked a second date for the concert a week later before everyone departed for the summer holidays. The following Sunday, the hors d'oeuvres were reassembled on platters, the bottles of wine and sparkling water were ready to be opened on the kitchen counter, and the chairs were neatly lined up in rows. The weather was co-operative, ensuring the temperature didn't expose the sensitive instruments to unnecessary heat and humidity.

Dobrochna suggested I once again speak first, then follow

up with my playing so I could enjoy the concert without fretting and worrying about my performance. Three years of practice had elapsed since my previous debut, and I felt the increased demands on myself. *I must perform better than when I played that simple minuet.* This time I'd be including a bit of vibrato, moving my fingers up and down the fingerboard from first to fourth positions, and adding more dynamics for colour and texture. I wanted to demonstrate my progress and was determined to make sure my gains were noticed.

I'd invited the next-door neighbours whose children were eager to attend. Six-year-old Quais in his shorts and shirt along with his four-year-old sister, Anaia, dressed in an orange and yellow sundress, slipped in through the side gate once they heard my voice addressing the guests. Quais occupied an empty chair beside the violist, while Anaia settled into one beside me.

On each seat, there was a program on coloured paper:

ENCHANTING MUSIC FOR A SUNDAY AFTERNOON
Sunday, June 26, 2022

Cellist: Dobrochna Zubek
Violist: Caitlin Boyle

Introduction: *The Enchantment of Listening II* (Mavis Himes)

Ludwig van Beethoven (1770–1827):
Eyeglasses Duo for Viola and Cello

Witold Lutosławski (1913–94): Duet "Bukoliki"

Reinhold Glière (1875–1956): Eight Pieces, Opus 39, for Violin and Cello (Arranged for Viola and Cello)

Johann Sebastian Bach (1685–1750):
Cello Suite No. 1 in G Major

Rebecca Clarke (1886–1979):
Two Pieces for Viola and Cello

By way of introduction, I once again gave a short presentation about the enchantment of music, elaborating on the atypical pairing of viola and cello and the history of music duets. Then I returned to my seat, and Dobrochna took the stage. "Once more, I'd like to welcome Mavis back to play some music. This will be a duet of her choosing from one of her music books." She then continued with some comments on my recent achievements in playing.

I heard the words but was already listening to my heart begin to thunder. I felt like a seven-year-old being discussed in the third person, as if in absentia. Finally, I heard some friends applaud and recognized my cue to get up.

While I'd felt quite self-assured about my playing on a final run-through in the morning, I was now caving into a case of nerves. But the first piece went well — a lovely duet from my *Piatti Étude for Two Cellos* book. *Relief.*

Then came the two pieces, easier in my estimation than the *Piatti* one, with their light step and straightforward melodies. Just in case, I'd prepared a third folk tune as an encore. In my state of nervous tension, I finished the second piece and immediately launched into the third, almost rushing my way to the finish line.

As if released from a blocked trapdoor, I almost ran back and collapsed into my seat. A gentle applause followed. Anaia smiled in my direction and reached out her hand to hold mine. My blood pressure lowered slowly with her gesture. Quais silently clapped his hands with a big grin.

Dobrochna then introduced the music to be played by the two professionals. And then the truly enthralling music of viola and cello commenced. Caitlin and Dobrochna played with effervescence and sparkle, pervading the open-air space. Beginning with Beethoven's Eyeglasses Duo, so humorously named to suggest the busy texture and difficult lines of the piece that required the donning of glasses, they showcased the unique yet complementary qualities of the cello and viola. Following with the fiery exuberance of Lutosławski's folkloric tune "Bukoliki" ("Bucolic") with its irregular patterns, we were introduced to Glière's Eight Pieces, a romantic yet structured composition with predictable and expressively long melodic lines. Dobrochna then treated us to a taste of Bach's cello suites. From the Baroque period, we jumped to the twentieth century to conclude with Rebecca Clarke's pieces with their soulful yet deceptive harmonies. Simply entrancing, enchanting, and transporting.

Quais and Anaia swayed in tandem and waved their hands to the beat of the first two pieces. Becoming restless, Quais then leaned over and asked if he could play my cello, and I whispered, "Later."

Compliments followed all around with accolades of "Encore, encore!"

"What a special performance."

"Amazing being so close to the musicians."

"Oh, Mavis, that was such a powerful concert."

Despite praise for the afternoon, I was hopelessly and completely dissatisfied by my performance. I hadn't expected perfection, but nor did I anticipate the interference of so much performance anxiety. I was sure I could play through my pieces with more power, more musicality, and more feeling. I could have accepted a few errors in intonation, but not such glaring finger misplacements.

I went to sleep questioning my desire to perform, even on the rare occasion, for friends or colleagues. That night I dreamed I lost my cello.

19

The Accident

On August 6, 2022, on a sunny Saturday, an unforeseeable encounter between my bicycle and a 2017 black Jeep Cherokee altered a chapter in my life.

A collision, an accident, a meeting of flesh and metal. Time, that engraver of memories, was permanently carved on my body that August day.

In and out of full consciousness, I remembered the siren of the ambulance followed by the arrival of my husband. I recalled the voices of the ambulance team — "Hi, my name's Emily. Hi, my name's Paul" — who informed me I'd be all right, that they were only permitted to give me Tylenol for pain, and that I'd be taken to a hospital. Still in my blood-stained pants and shirt, I was bundled onto a stretcher.

The ride was bumpy as I lay in the back of the clanging ambulance, thinking the suspension springs needed adjusting. I thought about who I had to notify. *Lois, yes, I must call Lois and tell her I won't make it to her art reception.*

The drive to Mount Sinai Hospital was followed by the hum of an overcrowded Emergency. "We'll try to escalate your case," Emily said as she wheeled my gurney against a wall lined with others. "Just let me check with a doctor."

Fortunately, or was it fortunate, the risk of infection with exposed bone placed me in a high-priority sequence. "Will I be able to play the cello?" I asked the first doctor who saw me.

Ignoring my query, he explained the next steps. "I'm

going to clean your arm immediately to prevent infection. Later today, you'll have surgery to repair your arm."

I heard "bone bath ... operation ... broken ... cast ... overnight" — the lexicon of the medical profession, the smiling faces of strangers, the dread of the body's vulnerability. I melted in and out of degrees of consciousness.

Five minutes or five hours went by after the cleansing procedure. I heard Lawlor say, "I'll see you later," and then he disappeared.

Another five minutes or five hours passed before I was wheeled several floors up and left alone along the wall of an empty corridor. More time crawled by, and I was returned downstairs. My surgery had been postponed, a euphemism for being bumped for a more critical emergency.

A great deal more time seemed to pass, and I was trundled upstairs once again and planted against the same wall. This time I was told by a nurse that my surgery would begin shortly. I asked if I could speak to Lawlor, since I knew he'd be waiting anxiously at home, expecting to hear I was already out of surgery.

When I was given a phone, I told my husband, "Surgery will be happening soon. A nurse will call you when I'm in recovery. Love you." The phone was then removed from my ear.

More hours inched by, and then I was finally rolled in to the freezer called an operating theatre. The clock above me read 9:00 p.m.

"The doctors have returned," a female nurse announced as a flurry of activity ensued. Before I knew it, several men and women hovered over me, pulling and shifting my position as if I were a corpse, prying and poking at different parts of my anatomy — my arm, fingers, neck, face.

Once again, I asked randomly to the roomful of people crowded about, "Will I be able to play the cello after surgery?"

"Of course," I heard someone say, chuckling as I drifted off.

Hours later I awoke to find myself in a hospital room. I learned from the nurse that I'd undergone a three-plus-hour operation in which my completely shattered elbow was reconstructed. My arm, cast from above my elbow to below my wrist in a ninety-degree angle, lay across my stomach. I'd agreed to an extra nerve-blocking anesthetic to minimize post-surgical pain for up to twelve hours and could hardly feel my fingers.

Alone in the hospital room, I felt time was playing me for a fool. I glanced at the clock high up on the wall facing me. It was an old-fashioned timepiece like the one I recalled at Hampstead Elementary School in Montreal. I closed my eyes and dropped off to sleep. Five minutes passed. I closed my eyes and dropped off to sleep. Five minutes passed once more. This pattern repeated itself throughout the night: 2:00 a.m., 3:00 a.m., 4:00 a.m. The minute hand ticked at what felt like a snail's pace, and I wondered if morning would ever arrive. Pain was minimal, but my mind raced with thoughts of my recovery. What about my cello? What about the trip to Banff scheduled in a few weeks? Thank God it wasn't my dominant arm. Thank God there was no concussion. Thank God it wasn't worse.

At one point, a nurse came in to monitor my vitals. Vitals equalled blood pressure, heartbeat, temperature — statistics that measured the body's functioning in real time. The nurse said I could get up to use the toilet. "No need for that bedpan," she chirped cheerily. She encouraged me to drink water, and I sipped melting ice cubes through a straw and waited for daylight to arrive.

Before I knew it, a surgeon gowned in medical greens was smiling down at me. "How are you feeling this morning? Can you move your fingers yet?"

I must have fallen asleep for a short time. I tried to wiggle my fingers and experienced some luck. He held my hand and asked me to apply pressure. "That was quite an operation. You sustained a very serious injury requiring a full break in the elbow. You now have three metal plates and a lot of screws supporting the bones. The issue will be straightening your arm by your side, but you'll have physiotherapy soon enough to help you deal with that."

What's soon enough? "Will I be able to play the cello again? How long do you think it'll take for my life to return to normal?" I knew my questions were unreasonable, but my mouth was uninhibited. Wooziness released me from rational considerations.

"Yes, you should be able to play the cello again," he responded very sensibly. "I can't tell you exactly when. That'll depend on your healing process. In the meantime, you'll be in a cast for the next two weeks and will be forced to take it easy. Then we'll see you back at the fracture clinic for X-rays and reassessment. You'll be given an appointment before you leave today."

Reasonable, calm, and measured, the surgeon wasn't too young to be arrogant nor too old to be cynical. He reassured me again that the cello would be in my future.

I avoided the question of time. I didn't want to blurt, *But it's urgent. I don't have lots of time. I need to get back to my practice or I might lose all my recent gains.*

I wanted to say I was a good healer, would work at it, would do all I was told to get better quickly. And I had to ask if that would make a difference. But instead I stared at my arm in heavy plaster and thought of Barbara Stevens's cast of signatures in our grade three classroom.

Before leaving, as he finished his notes, the doctor did an about-turn and said soothingly, "Now you have to rest. Your body's undergone a trauma. You need to give it *time* to heal."

When had that word *time* assumed such epic proportions?

A few hours later, Lawlor arrived to return me home.

Twenty-eight hours after leaving our house on my bicycle heading downtown for a date with a friend, I came back to our house with a paper bag of prescriptions, instructions for an emergency, an appointment card with a date in two weeks at the fracture clinic, and a reconstructed elbow in my left arm.

For the first forty-eight hours, I lay on the sofa, popping anti-inflammatories, Tylenol extra-strength, and hydromorphone tablets. I wanted to sleep but couldn't get comfortable.

"Time never stops, Mave," Lawlor said. "There's a time for everything. There's ER time, there's cast time, there's healing time, there's recovery time."

I shielded my ears. I didn't want to hear about the importance of letting the body mend itself. I was broken and had no energy. I lacked vitality. I was drained of those vitals measured by machines and monitors.

What I did know was that I had to play my instrument, but access to my therapeutic partner was denied and would continue to be so. I knew it would take time — not a comforting thought.

My days were long, my days were short. For the first week, I was glued to the sofa or the bed. Gradually, my energy returned as I noticed a decrease in pain and the need for pain-numbing meds. My elephant hand, puffy, bruised, and purple, began to shrink, and very slowly over the first two weeks, returned to normal.

I took my arm for short walks. It had become separate from me and the rest of my body, an appendage with a will and *volonté propre* — it didn't concede to my demands. The communication between my arm and the control centre in my brain had been temporarily severed: "This number is no longer in service."

We needed to become reacquainted. We had to find a new pathway of communication. When I fractured my arm in a ski accident at the age of sixteen, I'd worn a sling for several weeks. The fracture healed incorrectly in the area of my shoulder, permanently limiting my range of motion. This time, I reassured myself, my bones were broken and supported with hardware to ensure a correct resetting of the elbow.

One day, Enrique, a friend and a structural engineer by profession, chuckled. "Yes, of course, it's a structural design problem. I'd love to see the X-rays. Send them to me if you can."

I retreated from my music. I was unable to listen to or watch any music concerts, couldn't read any articles or books on music. I shut down. My body in its effort to mend itself sapped me of energy and inspiration.

Dobrochna was somewhere in the middle of the Pacific on a cruise with the Lincoln Center Orchestra. We'd arranged for me to study with Naomi Barron, another teacher, while Dobrochna worked on the cruise line for three months. Desperately, I wanted to contact her but didn't wish to disturb her with my news. If anything, I shunned most contacts.

Letter by letter with two fingers, I keyed in the word *patience* in the Google dictionary. *Patience:* "the capacity to accept or tolerate delay, trouble, or suffering without getting angry or upset; "bearing of a provocation, annoyance, misfortune, or pain without complaint, loss of temper; "an ability or willingness to suppress restlessness or annoyance when confronted with delay; "long-suffering, stoic, or tolerant."

How could one bear *misfortune* and *pain* without complaint or irritation? Was I merely to accept this intolerable situation? How could I move forward? I was no stoic.

I read: "Patience creates confidence, decisiveness, and a thoughtful outlook on life" and "Patience leads to wisdom and success." I learned that "silver-haired" described somebody who aged with beauty and grace, and that the qualities of patience and perseverance were typical silver-haired traits.

Not one person who knew me would ever use the adjective *patient* to describe me. No, they'd say, "Determined, motivated, and *very* impatient." I began to measure time in a different tempo: from three hours to the next pain pill to two weeks to cast removal, then six to eight weeks for bones to heal from a fracture. As it turned out, fractures took eight to twelve weeks or even longer to heal.

And while I was familiar with the experience of recovery from a fractured arm and major surgery for scoliosis as a teenager, I wasn't so sure how the healing process worked in the aging body of a septuagenarian. Did healing in an older person take longer as a matter of fact? Was I too embarrassed to ask anyone, or was I simply avoiding a condescending response? "Of course not, my dear." Or: "What did you expect? You're not a youngster anymore."

My friends told me to speak nicely to my arm lest it betray or punish me by refusing to co-operate. I frowned and cursed under my breath.

I was a realist. I knew that re-suturing of bones took time. I promised myself to be kind to my body and counted the days until I saw the doctor at the fracture clinic, anticipating a second, smaller cast plus a sling.

The night before my appointment, I couldn't sleep. Terrified to see the physical appearance of my arm with a railway track of staples and a protrusion of hardware like some monstrous appendage, I tossed and turned in bed. I worried about the deconditioning of my arm after two weeks of non-use. But most of all, I dreaded the potential breach in communication between my arm and brain. My last attempt to move my arm had been a total failure. Would the nerves now be restored to a secure and guaranteed contact?

There was a scene of chaos and pandemonium at the fracture clinic. The overworked receptionist repeated herself like a taped recording: "Line up on the left side. Have your health card ready. X-rays down the hall to the right. Have a seat and just wait your turn."

I was seen by Dr. Amit Anand, a young man with warm eyes and a welcoming smile who had been one of the four doctors present during my surgery. His assistant gently removed my cast and informed me he'd remove the staples, which might hurt. Every second staple incurred a loud and sharp *"Ouch!"* I closed my eyes before looking over to see my liberated limb. On top, it looked normal, but I couldn't see the injured underside.

"Okay, Mavis, now hold my hand." Dr. Anand brought me back from my thoughts. "Circle, squeeze, press, push down. Do you have sensation — here, here, and what about there?" He examined my arm from every angle. "You won't be recast, since the protocol now is to encourage arm activity through daily usage. You've already lost thirty percent function just from two weeks of cast immobility. We want you to get your arm moving again as soon as possible. You'll likely regain full functionality. Ten percent loss of full range of motion is most typical, but you won't even notice that slight limitation down the road. I'm pleased with the look of the incision, the decrease in swelling, and the positive kinesthetic sensations. All good signs of healing. Now let's get you seen for an X-ray.

No sooner had he said that, then I was whisked off down the corridor to the radiation department.

"That's a lot of hardware you have in your arm," the technician said. "Looks like it was a very complex break."

I wondered if I was supposed to say, "Thank you," as if I'd just been complimented on the state of my arm.

When I returned to see Dr. Anand, he showed me the X-ray images on his computer and further explained the findings I could barely comprehend any of it. All I knew was the importance of arranging physiotherapy as soon as possible and booking a return appointment to the clinic in another four weeks. Dr. Anand then wished me good luck and advised me to protect my arm in public spaces.

A conversation with a friend who also sported metal hardware embedded in her arm arranged for me to see her physiotherapist. A serendipitous cancellation in the physiotherapist's schedule resulted in an appointment one hour after my return from the hospital.

"You must be Carole's friend," the physiotherapist said as she approached me in the waiting room. "I knew it right away. Hi, my name's Charlotte Anderson."

A young woman with high-voltage energy extended her arm as I pondered her introductory comment. *You must be Carole's friend. Is it because I look so old? Is that why she knew me to be Carole's friend? There I go again, assuming everyone's thinking about my age.*

I followed Charlotte into the treatment room where she obtained the basic facts of my accident. After an extensive series of questions, she examined my arm thoroughly. "Wow, this is good," she said, as if speaking to an invisible colleague. "This is very good. I was expecting worse from what Carole told me. So pleased — the swelling, the incision, the movement already. I can see looking at your arm and observing your overall physical health that we've got this."

For the next forty-five minutes, Charlotte, my new best friend, manipulated my arm, discussed the treatment plan, and most importantly, reassured me of no permanent loss of function, even the ten percent mentioned by Dr. Anand. "And," she added as if reading my mind, "the cello will likely happen sooner than you think. But we'll have to see."

Then, as I readjusted my arm into the sling, its new home, Charlotte said in a very serious tone, "This is going to involve work, pain, and effort. The physio exercises I'll send you later today need to be done daily, and I promise to work with you through some *ouch* to get you back to *your* normal. Perhaps you might want to take some Tylenol before your physio sessions."

I left my first physiotherapy session buoyant, finally convinced I'd be able to reconnect with Simone, even if it meant waiting a while to get there. I committed to pursuing my physiotherapy diligently, both the home exercises and the twice-weekly sessions in person to start. That evening, I received an email with a video program of specific exercises and a list of do's and don'ts. At the end of the email, Charlotte wrote: "We got this. I'm here for you."

My measurement of time changed once again. I now calculated it by the extensions and flexions I could perform with my arm, the number of repetitions, the range of motion. Within one week, I could bend my arm five centimetres closer to my shoulder than the previous week. I could begin to touch my forehead and my hair, put on a pair of earrings unassisted if I bent my head forward, take off my pants without any *ouch* reaction, tie up a pair of runners.

For the first two weeks, I couldn't carry anything heavier than a teacup, push open a heavy door, chop or cut an apple or melon, slice a zucchini, make the bed or clean a sink. Lawlor took over the household chores without complaint.

Four weeks after the accident, I decided to have a conversation with Simone. I pulled her out, lay the fingerboard against my chest, and straddled my knees on either side of her. My music stand off to one side, I picked up my bow and tuned her with my iPhone app. I played some very slow bowings with my right arm on open strings that required no left-arm movement. My eyes teared as I experienced the strong resonance of sound inside my entire body. *We're back, Simone. We'll get there, my sweetheart. Just be patient.*

On September 17, six weeks and two days after my accident, I had my first cello lesson with Naomi. We met at

Heinl's in one of the practice rooms on the second floor. Naomi and I had already gotten together at my place prior to Dobrochna's departure, and I'd sensed a certain calmness in her manner, a contrast to Dobrochna's more explosive and big personality. I knew I could be vulnerable with Naomi and open to her suggestions.

However, despite the resumption of lessons, Charlotte only granted me permission to use my right arm. When I brought my cello to physiotherapy, she explained that cello playing was the *marathon*, and we must build up to this event by gradually introducing partial muscle groups. The elbow being the epicentre of my physical trauma, it was necessary to worry about all the soft tissue — tendons, muscles, ligaments — supporting the bones. Charlotte told me, "That's my job — to monitor your progress and help strengthen all those things around the bones. But go *crazy* with your right arm."

Very gradually over the next few weeks, my repertoire of permissible playing expanded. I was allowed to play one scale three times, then one scale ten times, then more scales were added until finally I was playing simple pieces from my earlier *Suzuki* and *Piatti* books, at least those without any extensions or complex positions.

Once again, I was rewarded for my focused attention and physio commitment. Everyone was pleased with my progress — the surgeon, the physiotherapist, the massage therapist, my friends. All were shocked by my rate of recovery and how far I'd come in a relatively short time.

"You're breaking records, Mavis," Charlotte insisted in her typically positive manner. You're doing amazingly well."

And I wondered if what they weren't saying was "for your age." Yet I, too, was pleased with my incremental advancement.

20

Setback

Satisfied with the expanding activities of my left arm, I decided it was time, as well as *the* time of year, to host another Ladies' Lunch on November 22, 2022. For more than twenty five years, this annual tradition of gathering and feasting had become a ritual at my house. This one would be the first after two years of virtual meetings during the pandemic. I wanted to celebrate with my friends and share our laughter once again, so I threw myself wholeheartedly into the preparations.

Hugs and kisses took place with each person's arrival. Ann showed off her fancy new sweater coat with an embroidered pattern of a horse as she stepped through the front door. Pat impressed us with her new scarf gifted her by the young designer in her building who imported goods from India and Nepal. We admired and complimented each other on the seamless transition we were making after the imposed isolation of Covid.

Carrying our plates heaped with an assortment of leafy greens, colourful casseroles, and crispy breads from the kitchen counter buffet, we assembled ourselves around the dining room where we picked up conversations dropped during our culinary intermission.

"A toast to our wounded but recovered warrior hostess!" my friends exclaimed.

As usual, we meandered in and out of different topics, lapsing into musings and reminiscences. It started with

Carol, a newer member of the sisterhood, asking how long we'd been meeting. I pulled out the photo album begun three years into our get-togethers.

Everyone chirped, commenting on the clothes, hairdos, and visible changes.

"Wow, look at us!" Pat said.

"Oh, my God, no kidding," Ann added. "Don't we look great! Just like today. No different." And everyone cheered.

"But really," Andrea said, "isn't it amazing how quickly time flies? We've been meeting for over twenty-five years and yet it hardly feels like that despite all the shit and stuff that's happened."

"And most of us are now retired and doing other things than our old jobs," Pat said.

Pearl and Ana, both working in the field of mental health, reminded everyone of that special aura of wisdom surrounding aging therapists. "Classrooms and auditoriums are filled to brimming when a senior analyst or therapist gives a keynote address," Pearl noted. "Irrespective of stooped posture and trembling hands, the old ones are revered as wizened masters."

I laughed. "There you go. Respect, please. I'm now one of those masters!"

"A toast to maturity, wisdom, and old age!" Ann cried.

"Well, you know that time's an artificial construct," Deborah with her calm voice and serene manner spoke up. "There's no such thing as objective time. We humans created time and measure it with our watches and clocks. Prehistoric man didn't look at his wrist or iPhone all day to verify the time. He looked up at the heavens and checked the land to determine the cycles of days and nights and the seasons."

"Do continue the lecture, oh wise one," Pat quipped, while others looked skeptically askance, not quite convinced.

Becoming serious, I, too, shared with the women how I'd always felt. "I believe we have both an internal subjective age and an empirical chronological age. The interior one, private and self-reflective, is the one in which we retain an image of the self we once were, like an idealized memory redeeming all the wrinkles, aging spots, unwanted hair follicles under the chin. And that's the one we inhabit despite our external appearances. This ideal age persistently lags behind our actual age, the one we wish to dispel, the one we sometimes banish from everyday thinking. So, for example, when I was forty, I felt as if I was twenty. I mixed with people thinking we were on the same level. Then when I was fifty, I felt as if I was thirty-five. Now, the gap feels as if it's narrowing. I'm not suggesting this is an original thought, but that's how it seems to me."

Carolyn piped up. "I totally agree. I'm still that twenty-year-old inside."

"That's delusional!" Andrea disagreed.

"No, I'm with you, Mavis," Pat interjected. "I'm still twenty-two inside, the year I met the first love of my life. I think I just want to stay that age forever."

"Really, you'd go back to that time and do it all over again?" Ann scoffed. "Are you nuts?"

Laughter and tears ensued as we each reached back into our memory bank of experiences, numbers of ages flying around like a canvas of Marc Chagall figures.

"That was the best Ladies' Lunch in years," I said as my friends packed up their doggy bags of treats and headed out the door. "So great to finally see each other after the past couple of years."

That evening, I reflected on the day, sharing my thoughts with Lawlor. Time in the theatre of life had certainly carried us women along all those years. We each had made choices, entering and exiting multiple scenes of shared experiences — children, divorce, career changes, grandchildren, menopause, retirement planning, loss of parents, and even the passing of partners. Each act was full and challenging, yet we all participated to our fullest. Despite our differences and arguments — was time circular or linear, subjective or objective, artificially constructed or genetically primed? — we still could spend an afternoon together when time stood still for a few hours.

Three days later, on November 25, 2022, my arm began to feel strange. Painful and swollen around my elbow, fingers unable to function easily, I felt the dreaded sensation of disconnection. I knew I'd pushed my arm with all the arrangements demanded for the Ladies' Lunch. That busy weekend of physical activity was followed by my online Pilates class on Monday and a twenty-minute cello practice.

By Wednesday, I couldn't use my left arm or hand. Weak and sore, the dreaded sensation of a brain-to-arm faulty connection reappeared every time I tried to tie my shoelaces or do up a zipper. I couldn't push open a lightweight door or brush my teeth without a strange tingling in my fingers and a total lack of strength. Based on the significant deterioration in my range of motion, this was a huge step backward in my recovery.

Something was unquestionably wrong. I tried to book an appointment with Charlotte, but she was out of town — the woman who *never* took a holiday and was a complete workaholic, available basically 24/7 for her patients. As my range of motion diminished, I emailed Charlotte and explained my symptoms. She called me from New York City at 11:00 p.m. on a Friday night.

Over the phone, she asked me a series of questions and quickly ruled out any need to be seen in Emergency. I could still move my hands and arms in critical ways, and no severe throbbing, sharp chronic pain, or spasms in my elbow. Charlotte suggested it was likely muscle pain from the weekend hustle and bustle. I wasn't convinced, sensing something far less benign than muscle strain.

"I'll see you in my office on Tuesday, Charlotte told me. "Due diligence, you should get an X-ray."

In desperation, I booked an emergency appointment at the fracture clinic. Dr. Anand wouldn't be there the day I was scheduled, but I insisted on the soonest slot available. An unfamiliar doctor met me in the curtained cubicle after my X-rays. From his expression, I knew the news wasn't good. With a frown, he uttered a medley of words: "Broken metal, broken bone, a non-union or delayed union, no more activities, possible future break, more surgery possible."

Stop! Stop! I indicated with my good arm. *Bombardment!*

Everything stopped. Everything had to stop. I was stopped in my tracks.

Only when I asked him to repeat things slowly did I begin to process what had happened. Recurrent motion of my elbow and arm had caused a break in the metal supporting one of the many broken bones in my arm. The location was a challenging one for healing, and as the doctor explained, a non-union or persistent fracture wasn't uncommon. He mentioned a bone-stimulator device, "very expensive if you don't have insurance," that helped with bone growth. If I wished, he could write me a script.

Too shocked to respond, he left me with a few instructions: "Don't carry anything more than a teacup for a few weeks, don't strain your arm, and come back for an X-ray in twelve weeks."

I left the hospital in a haze. *Are you kidding me? That's it? No further direction than that? What could I do? What should I do?* No cello playing was obvious — I couldn't even bend my arm and touch my shoulder, let alone come close to reaching the left-arm cello position.

I felt a plunge into darkness. *It was my fault. I overdid it. I was too impatient. I pushed too much. I never know when to stop.* And yet a part of me believed I'd been trying to pace myself according to my arm's feedback.

Another appointment with Dr. Anand was arranged for a

few days later. The surgeon, shocked by this incident, tried to hide his dismay. "You were doing so well. I told others about your stellar progress. I gave you the green light to go ahead and resume your life myself, including your cello playing. What a disturbing turn of events."

When I arrived at Dr. Anand's office, he sat down with me in front of two sets of X-rays — current and previous. He'd spoken to the other physician I'd seen earlier and explained what he thought had happened, concluding by reassuring me that it wasn't my fault. "This is biology. It's the wear and tear of movement creating a non-union between bone and metal. This is *not* your fault. Besides, you're the psychologist, after all! You know self-blame is damaging."

He encouraged me to keep some movement to engage the muscles but to curtail any activities putting strain on the arm for four weeks — in other words, I could basically do nothing. Then he ordered more X-rays and a reassessment in four weeks.

I was encouraged to try the bone-strengthening device, which I purchased with insurance funds. Every night I religiously wrapped the device around my arm for thirty minutes. It sent out electromagnetic waves to help build back bone mass.

Charlotte seemed a bit downcast when I saw her next. I felt as if I'd disappointed everyone, but most of all myself. "Mavis, we've still got this. This is a blip. Temporary. We'll get you there. You can't get rid of me that easily. I'm here to the end of your return to normal functioning. *Your normal*, which includes the cello and all your other activities."

Like Dr. Anand, she told me not to aggravate my arm: no lifting, no carrying, no cooking, no washing. I didn't need to be told; my arm wouldn't co-operate whatsoever.

Not to be consoled, I lost confidence, appetite, determination, and most of all, hope. I couldn't rid myself of guilt, convinced I'd brought this on myself by my overzealousness and determination to return to normal. While Dr. Anand, the bone-device technician, and others said — "it's all about the biology, bone non-union happens in a percentage of cases due to the complexities of movement" — I couldn't bring myself to digest that information.

Physiotherapy began with a return to one-pound weights. Progress needed to be rebuilt back. *Build back better*, I heard in my head. Recovery time once again made me do its bidding. I was no longer an agent of my own destiny; my bones would recuperate and strengthen within their own timeline.

Simone lay on her stand, bemoaning her lack of contact. Occasionally, I pretended to play, taking out my cello bench and wrapping my arms around her. One day, I decided to try a scale. *Ouch — no, not ready for that yet.*

After weeks of enforced stillness, my arm started to return to its former self — less swelling, less heat, more strength, more mobility. My weights increased, my activities intensified, my confidence grew. Still reluctant to push myself, I was truly learning the art of patience.

Dobrochna returned to Toronto just prior to the Christmas holidays and wasn't aware of my setback. We agreed to meet at our local haunt in January 2023 after seasonal festivities settled down. With coloured gift bags in hand, we greeted each other like long-lost friends. We cried and laughed at the unpredictable peregrinations and meanderings of our lives.

"I'm still not allowed to touch my cello despite the gains I've made," I informed her. "We need to prep the foundational patterning of movement before we add more weight and cello. Remember? It's the marathon that we're still in training for," I said, echoing Charlotte's words.

"You must take all the time you need," Dobrochna told me. "Trust muscle memory. You'll be surprised at what you've retained from before. All's not lost, Mavis."

After we parted, I had follow-up X-rays to be taken. These revealed a non-union of the fracture. My family physician now ordered a bone-density test for me. *But this was an impact fracture!* I wanted to scream.

Finally, ten weeks after the Ladies' Lunch and the acute setback, Charlotte announced I was ready to begin playing the cello again. "Five minutes. One scale only. You can go crazy with your right arm, and up to a two or three on the *ouch* scale. Anything more than that and you stop immediately! Deal? And ten minutes icing after each practice."

I paid close attention to my arm, micro-analyzing every sensation. Did this hurt? Was this too much? Was this a two or a three *ouch*? I was reluctant to push limits. Instead, I approached my return much more cautiously, heeding Charlotte's advice.

Expanding my scales and some of the exercises and études I'd been practising with Naomi in the fall, I tried to play the one new piece we'd started: Felix Mendelssohn's "On Wings of Song" and the Catalan tune "El cant dels ocells ("Song of the Birds"), both at a Royal Conservatory of Music Level 5 repertoire.

Feeling good strength in my arm, and with virtually no ache or discomfort, I pulled out some music pieces played prior to my injury: a Bach and a Tchaikovsky from *Suzuki Book 4*. My fingers initially tripped on themselves, but after one or two attempts, I could retrace the melody through my finger memory. Dobrochna was correct — all wasn't lost.

I had one more appointment at the fracture clinic. "Hi, Tatiana, I guess this is the last time you'll be seeing me," I jokingly said to the calm receptionist keeping the parade of us with broken shoulders, elbow, knees, and hips on track and in time. We were now on a first-name basis.

Shuffling down the hall for my X-ray, I returned to the curtained cubicle to wait for Dr. Anand. When he appeared, I showered him with positive comments about my arm, its multiple gains and improvements, demonstrating against the hospital gurney how I could do a plank on hands and knees, lifting my right hand to fully weight-bear on my left.

"Well, I hate to say this. But the X-rays tell a different story, Mavis."

"What? You must be joking!"

"Come and I'll show you the X-rays," he said, leading me to a computer screen. Sure enough, a fuzzy area suggested an incomplete fracture healing.

While I was shocked and in disbelief, we reviewed the options. I agreed to have a CT scan, which would provide a much clearer image of the elbow from all angles. Then we'd decide on the next steps. In the meantime, I was to continue all my activities and follow the advice of my physiotherapist.

Paradoxically, my functional behaviour was now in complete contrast with the radiographic images of my body. I spoke to the technician, Bob, from whom I'd bought the bone stimulator. He advised me to continue with my device, since the X-rays had shown significant new bone growth, even if not at the fracture line. Bob reminded me how all the other tears and fissures and broken bones had mended — only one persistent fracture remained. In the meantime, I was getting stronger and stronger and had surpassed my range of motion prior to the setback.

Three weeks later, Charlotte announced, "Green light for a cello lesson."

I was overjoyed. This was now the *right time*.

21

Return to the Cello

Dobrochna insisted that our first lesson after such a long break should be at my house. Prior to her trip, we'd been alternating.

The night before, a jittery sensation set into my stomach. How would the lesson go? Would I be able to demonstrate the gains I had made in bowings with my right arm? Would she see the improvement in intonation that I discovered in spite of the long hiatus in our lessons?

I figured the questions I should have been asking were: "And why did I still need to impress my teacher? Did one ever get over those demonic childhood voices? I certainly didn't need my patients to remind me that the inner world respects no boundaries of time. Nor did it consider past, present, or future.

Arriving punctually, I heard her signature boots on the front porch as I warmed up on scales. As soon as Dobrochna opened the door, I hit the wrong note. *Of course.*

We hugged each other warmly. "Can I see your arm?" Dobrochna asked me. "And see some movements? When I was wrapped around Simone, she examined my left-arm position, circling my seat like an adjudicator at a dog show. "Okay, now let's tune our instruments." It was the familiar refrain at the beginning of each lesson.

Attentive to my injury and my potential for discomfort, alongside my desire to return to playing, we very slowly covered some old and new groundwork. I was thrilled to hear Dobrochna say my left-arm placement hadn't been impacted in any negative way by the injury.

She asked to hear some warm-up exercises, new scales, and a few simple pieces. "Your hand and arm muscles are now ready to move to the next level," she said as she moved my fingers deeper and more C-shaped on the fingerboard. "That's it. Now notice the difference in your sound." Minor adjustments created major improvements in sound quality and production.

For the first few weeks, Dobrochna suggested I return to simple folk pieces for cello duets we'd performed at the summer concert, in addition to some simple technical études.

By this time, my practice was up to twenty or twenty-five minutes with little to no pain in my elbow. Charlotte was concerned about the possibility of developing tendonitis at the elbow joint; the unhealed bone fracture was now of no concern to her despite the last X-ray. "You'll see. It'll all be fine on the scan. X-rays always lag bone growth. Bob also mentioned the same thing."

I was pumped and enlivened. But I wasn't oblivious to the physical changes resulting from my accident: the deformed resting position of my arm against my leg, the jagged scar and knobby metal protrusions, the sensation of metal under my arm while working at my desk, the altered sleep position on my favoured side, and the uniquely awkward sensations in all my arm movements. However, I felt tremendous gratitude that I could play the cello, tie my shoelaces, bake and wash, and perform all those daily activities without any *ouch*. Two weeks later, I had increased my practice time to almost thirty minutes and very gradually returned to my pre-accident rhythm with Simone.

Forced to slow down and limit myself to playing in shorter time frames that were technically easier to allow my arm to heal, I became aware of striking shifts in my attitude and perspective toward cello playing. I noticed the extent to which I was focused on the sound of my playing, as if

I could step outside my body and hear myself play. Instead of pushing ahead with grit and resolve, I allowed myself to hear the sounds produced by me and my cello. More relaxed, my body very naturally swayed with Simone, and I appreciated the beauty of her voice. Sinking into the strings and the fingerboard brought out a fullness and mellowness I hadn't previously detected in my playing. When I played Tchaikovsky's "Chanson triste," Opus 40, No. 2, *largo*, a tempo more suitable for the current level of my arm, an increased space for true depth of resonance appeared to open up.

I realized the extent to which my learning had been accomplishment and progress — advancing to the next level, mastering the next technical step — without appreciating the time required for my muscles to build and flex or extend in ways they couldn't have done without the developmental growth over the years.

Gradually, I accepted the musical status I'd achieved. This new insight made me realize my determination and zealousness, always considered assets, could also be a handicap or liability, interfering with my pleasure to play simple pieces and be captivated by my own playing. By accepting the level I'd attained, I could recognize my slow but steady progress.

Not surprisingly, my early years of learning had been dominated by the mastery of intonation. Without hitting the right notes, there could never be musical rendering of a composer's intention, even though as students we were also introduced to the dynamics and phrasing, the colours and textures of sound that characterized the musical greats.

While I'd always wanted to introduce more musical expression and dynamics into my playing, I'd also been more concerned, not surprisingly, to hit the correct notes. And yet, in my haste to advance, I hadn't permitted myself time to develop the depth of sound, dynamic modulations, and phrasings I cherished in my favourite musicians. That required additional time.

MAVIS HIMES

As my arms returned to mould around Simone's slender frame, I was learning that to reach her heart and to become the best cellist I could be, I had to incorporate both technique and musical expression "in time."

The appointment for my CT scan arrived surprisingly quickly, given I was told I might have to wait months. Charlotte and I joked about this final opportunity to see the handsome Dr. Anand. I'd mentioned to my friends that my progress and lack of pain made this appointment a question of due diligence on the part of the medical team. I looked forward to no more hospital visits regarding my arm.

Once again, I strode down the familiar corridor of the fifth floor at Mount Sinai Hospital still under construction, passed the plastic window divider behind which Tatiana with her still-masked face welcomed the injured to the fracture clinic, and on to the imaging department, also still undergoing renovation.

In my head, I latched on to the music of Florence Price, a twentieth-century American composer and influential figure in Chicago's Black Renaissance whose piece *Adoration* I was now studying in an arrangement for piano and cello. As the lyrical melody pulsed within me, I safely withdrew from the medical environment and listened to a rendition of cellist Laura Andrade on cello and pianist Michelle Schumann interpret this duet.

When my name was called, I surrendered to the machine designed like a spaceship from which I knew a computer would generate three-dimensional images of my elbow in a jigsaw of positions. Soundless and sensation-less, I felt as if some sort of revelation determining my fate would be rendered by this non-invasive, galactic-looking device.

By week's end, I was back for my follow-up appointment to discuss test results. I sat in the cubicle of the fracture clinic, positive that my recent gains in strength and move-ment would mean a short but concise visit.

Tatiana had already informed me that Dr. Anand was no longer holding fracture clinic hours, so I was prepared to be seen by someone new. I waited patiently reading my book as I tried not to eavesdrop on the familiar words uttered around me: "Yes, the X-rays show your fracture is coming along and healing well. You're now ready for physiotherapy, and it's critical that you follow the exercises given you by your ther-apist. I'd like to see you back here in another six weeks." What had seemed so distinctive seven months earlier now sounded routine and uneventful.

I was greeted by another young physician, chart in hand, with what I assumed was my test results, but then thought he must have made a mistake when he immediately proclaimed, "The one fracture in your elbow hasn't healed, the one where the metal broke ..." And his voice trailed off as I stopped listening for a few seconds. "You'll *likely* require another surgery, since this fracture that runs from here to here," he said as he drew a line across my upper arm from the front to the back five centimetres above my elbow joint, as if slicing a piece of meat. "Normal wear and tear will most *probably* cause it to give way. You're fine now, but these things *usually* don't last without repair."

Likely? Probably? Usually? What were the statistics? Where were the studies? *When? How long?* What was the measure of time being using? Were we talking weeks, months, years?

Sensing my concerns, the doctor suggested he show me the results of the scan and X-rays. Pointing to the images on the computer, he tried to explain, using everyday language interspersed with some technical terms, the prognosis for my arm. Knowing I wouldn't remember accurately, I asked him to repeat everything at least twice.

"Have I got this right? The bone break, this distal humerus fracture, the lower end of the upper-arm bone here, can't be trusted to hold if the metal plate breaks any further ... and this will inevitably occur one day? Yet, in the normal course of things, you expect the metal won't last forever as long as the bone heals sufficiently?"

"Correct," the doctor said. "And bone usually heals within three to four months."

"And you're saying that in my case the fracture hasn't healed, and it's been over six months? *A non-union* fracture, as you call it. Is it due to my age? Do I have old bones or something?"

"No," the physician once again reassured me. "In your case, it's most likely the exposed bone at the time of injury that put you at higher risk for a non-union."

Here I was at the mercy of my treatment doctors to give me some direction. I wanted answers and sought certainty in those replied, not statistics and possibilities.

I left with my head swarming with questions: What do I do now? Lead my life? Back off activities? Resume normal functioning? And how was that possible when told my fracture might give out on me one day?

The new doctor gave me the name of an orthopedic surgeon specializing in non-union fractures. When I was told it would take time to get an appointment, I refused to ask *how much*. I was left with the impression this next specialist, aggressive in his approach, would likely recommend a revision surgery. I assumed that would be a touch-up, but when I asked specifically what it would entail, I was informed it would require a full redo with bone grafting to help seal the fracture.

When I walked out of the hospital, I called Lawlor. He didn't need me to say anything; he heard my long and audible exhalation.

I didn't know how long I'd have to wait for my appointment with Dr. Aaron Nauth, my new specialist. After all, patience wasn't my strongest attribute.

At the end of my workday, I embraced Simone, and we sang together for thirty-six minutes.

The silence and invisibility of my fracture remained a mystery to me. How could my arm not be healing when I had no pain or discomfort?

A few weeks after that hospital visit and prior to my consultation with the specialist, encouraged by my musical progress, I decided to return to a piece of music I'd played before the injury: the Allegro from the *Sonata in C Major*, Opus 40, No. 1, by the French cellist Jean-Baptiste Bréval. I told myself, that if the fracture was going to give way, let it happen on my time while I was doing something pleasurable.

I played through the two pages of music with the introductory double stops, the varied tempos, and the multiple triplets in quick succession. My fingers tripped along, and I felt my arm become increasingly tired. I pushed myself but couldn't make it to the end of the piece without strain in my muscles and tendons.

At my next lesson, I told Dobrochna about my unsuccessful attempt. "I must 'fess up here, D," I announced sheepishly. "I tried to play through the Bréval, but the truth is I couldn't manage it. I guess you were right about my not being ready for that one."

"Don't you trust me?" she asked.

I couldn't read her expression.

"You and I have been gradually building up your stamina and strength," she continued. "We started with half a page of music, then a full page, and now a page plus a few lines. Your arm still needs time to build itself back up to where you were."

"Yes, you're absolutely correct," I replied. Feeling reprimanded for acting like a peevish child, I agreed to follow her more reasonable timetable.

She laughed and hugged me. "Welcome back, Mavis!"

Despite the questionable results of my arm's healing, I continued my usual practice and learned some new pieces while simultaneously guarding against an overabundance of effort. Eight weeks later, I found myself once again in the waiting room of another downtown hospital. And once more I was told that further X-rays of my arm were required. And once again the commentary by a hyper-energetic technician: "That's quite the hardware you have there."

An orthopedic physician completing his fellowship at this teaching hospital spent forty-five minutes with me as I described the accident, the recovery, the setback, and the current activities I was able to pursue. All I wanted to know was whether the persistent fracture would heal, and if not, what would be recommended. I'd spent eight weeks on a teeter-totter of saying yes/no to potential surgery.

"I'll discuss all of this with Dr. Nauth," he told me, "and we'll both return in a few minutes."

And without any further comment, he left me alone in the cubicle of an office stacked with boxes of disinfectant, gauze pads, and blue surgical gloves. I leaned back in the stackable vinyl chair, a prototype with which I'd become all too familiar, pulled out my book, and waited for Dr. Nauth and his colleague to appear.

When he entered the cubicle, Dr. Nauth, this so-called guru of non-unions, looked at me and then at the papers in his hand. With succinctness, he said, "I've just reviewed your file with my colleague who you've already met, and according to the X-rays we took this afternoon, I'd say your fracture's healing nicely."

Before I had time to unfold the paper with my list of questions on my lap — "If this scenario, then what … if that scenario, then what" — Dr. Nauth immediately answered the query that had kept me mumbling numbers in reverse, tallying my breaths, and even counting godforsaken sheep in the early hours of the morning when most people were asleep.

"There's absolutely no need for surgery, for revision surgery to be exact. Your arm seems to be healing when compared even to the X-rays from two months ago. You can continue with everything — no restrictions of activity."

"And my cello playing?"

"Yes, including your cello playing. However, I'd like to see you again in three months just to be sure."

Restraining myself from giving him a huge embrace, as if he'd had something to do with these positive results, I lifted my sheet of questions. "Is there anything I can do to damage my arm? Is there anything I can do to hasten the healing?"

"As I said, no restrictions. Keep up whatever you've been doing. And *if*, perchance, something happens and you feel pain in your arm at any time, then call me directly through the clinic number. Now when you leave, make sure you book your follow-up for three months."

The mysterious workings of the body, the fallibility of test results — I wasn't about to question the radical conversion from being told quite definitely that one of the fractures in my injured elbow was considered a non-union that would likely require further revision surgery to being advised all was well in my limb. Like a damaged tree, I was convinced I'd be left with an ugly, gnarled knot where I'd been sliced and cut.

Immediately, I called Lawlor with the good news, and we celebrated with a toast of *vino rosso* that evening.

Two weeks later, I presented myself back in Charlotte's pristine office, with her mobile skeleton and assortment of coloured dumbbells. Anticipating her wish to hear my results, I blurted out the wonderful news from the surgeon. "He said, 'Healing's happening. No evidence of a non-union fracture. No restrictions on activities. All's good.'"

"I knew it!" she exploded. "I knew it!"

"But I have an even bigger surprise for you today," I added coyly. "Want to guess?"

Charlotte wasted no time engaging in guessing games. "I give up. What is it?"

Tears welling in my eyes, I proudly announced, "I bicycled to my appointment today. I just had my bike serviced and this was the first time I've ridden it. I bicycled to this appointment on the very same red bike from my accident."

Charlotte pulled me into an embrace, tears matching mine on her cheeks. "Oh, Mavis. I'm so happy for you and so proud of you. You've made my day."

"I admit I was nervous and hyper-vigilant as I rode here … but I did it!"

"You know, Mavis, this was the one thing I wasn't sure about with your recovery. I knew your arm would heal, but I always wondered about the psychological impact on your getting back on the bike. It could've gone either way, but I'm truly pleased about your progress. Good on you!"

22

Summing Up

I stared at my computer and eyed the powerful presence of the mature maple tree that stood out against the background of my screen. In the foreground, facing an audience-filled small auditorium, was a cellist playing Bach's Cello Suite No. 2 in D Minor. I watched and listened as the young woman swayed with her instrument, eyes closed, as if communing with someone invisible to the rest of us. At the probing and introspective prelude, my own thoughts were filled with a brooding darkness that transformed over the course of the piece into a lightness carried by the speed and energy of the final gigue.

For eight weeks in the spring of 2023, I participated in an online program entitled "Music Art Life: Unlocking Meaning and Finding Purpose." Facilitated by Yo-Yo Ma, registered participants could attend group discussions, performances of each of Bach's cello suites, and guest lectures by speakers from a variety of disciplines covering themes such as life and music, creativity and community, framed around the suites.

Musicians and non-musicians alike debated and engaged with the musical material of the suites as a way of weaving and exchanging viewpoints on life and performance. "Good technique is playing without thinking," one cellist replied to Yo-Yo's question on craft. "We all try so hard to play with so many rules and tricks, but ultimately, one needs to throw it all away, own the moment, and play without thinking."

Other comments from the participants included:

- "Your life *is* your art form. Everybody's an artist no matter what your lifestyle. Each person chooses their own form of artistic expression, be it in their work, their appearance, or whatever."
- "I think it's important *not* to think of perfection. It just gets in the way. Perfection is death. Living is never perfect."
- "I think of performing in the same way I think of giving a party. I'm celebrating with others, exchanging the pleasures of my music and artistry."
- "Musicians have a gift to share with others. Our listeners don't care whether we hit the right note or slide through a glissando. I'm convinced it's more about the impact of music on people."

Yo-Yo enlarged on these comments by reminding cellists of the importance of, and even the responsibility of, sharing their gifts of performance as a way of passing on their excitement and imagination to others. "In this way," he concluded, "we can pass on the joy we derive from our playing to our listeners who, in turn, can pass their pleasure on to others. If music is meaningful, it deserves to be remembered, and it's our job to ignite that passion in others."

As I listened to the words of Yo-Yo, whose humanity and compassion, generosity and humility, have brought music and especially the cello repertoire to millions of people globally, I recognized the substance and urgency of what he was saying. The musician was a mediator, a guide who provoked questions and invited listeners to participate in a journey. And as with involvement in any adventure, expectations of surprise and tenderness, rapture and anguish, awaited those who opened themselves to the experience. A great musician was also a shaman capable of entrancing and enchanting people into otherworldly realms.

For an instant, I was transported to the atrium of Princess Margaret Hospital, a major cancer centre in Toronto hosting regular musical recitals of all genres. Suddenly, I recalled the softening faces of patients hooked up to machines and smiles bursting like sunrays through a cloudburst while attending a jazz or classical concert. I remembered the shaking hands of a white-haired octogenarian grimacing from pain only to observe her tapping her nobbled fingers on her lap, head shifting from side to side once the music began.

And I recollected the words of Dr. SarahRose Black, a music therapist participating in a panel on music, health, and well-being at the same hospital. "We're musical beings," she'd asserted, tapping her hands on her chest repeatedly. "Our heartbeat is a drum, and the first sound heard by a fetus is this heartbeat in utero."

Traversing the stage in rhythmic steps, she'd continued. "Now, imagine that regular pulse, steady and hypnotic. Hear it inside you. Then, consider the musical language of dialogue, beginning with the coos and babbles of a primitive code between mother and child. Imagine the elaboration of words and sentences that form the foundation of our human communication. And finally, envision the lullabies, the first organized tunes an infant hears."

At the end of the online workshop, I silently vowed that I, too, would one day create those spontaneous sparks and contours hidden within musical notes. I, too, would arouse curiosity and interest in an audience by bringing music to life. After all, scientific studies had already shown how music stimulated and activated regions of the brain that controlled movement so that we were literally *moved by music.*

For me, music inspired, captivated, and enchanted. In the silence of my music space, I was moved by what physicists would say was sound organized into the structure of music, what neuroscientists would determine was the activation of the pleasure-reward circuitry in the brain increasing my levels of dopamine like a mood-enhancing drug, what musicologists would declare was the conflict and resolution of anticipated harmonies and rhythms, and what the Ancients would pronounce was an embodiment of the beatific and the exalted, a manifestation of the divine.

As the summer of 2023 approached, I began to anticipate the break from Dobrochna. She was off to Poland while I took my holidays later in September. Before she departed, we discussed options for a substitute teacher or for long-distance Zoom lessons.

"I've been feeling a stronger connection with my playing," I noted, wondering if she also recognized the change.

"I can see the improvement, as well," she agreed.

I knew my injury had forced my overall tempo to *ritardando* and recognized that by slowing down and accepting the pace my body demanded, I was paradoxically advancing quicker.

Repeating technical points and recommendations made years earlier had begun to coalesce. New and old directives had been translated into performance with stronger sound and better intonation. I heard Dobrochna's voice internalized: *While bowing, think horizontal, not vertical. Unfold and fold back without stopping your bow. Keep moving with more anticipation of the next movement and position. Your left hand needs more weight, more sinking into the strings. Pay attention to your elbow height when you do string-crossings.*

What had seemed impossible and unsustainable months and years ago was becoming incorporated into my movement repertoire. My return to the basics with more patience and less urgency was clearly making a difference.

In addition to my private lessons, Dobrochna and I considered the possibilities of my playing with others in an amateur string trio or quartet. While an earlier attempt had been made to pair me with another cello student and Dobrochna, the logistics had proven too complicated.

Instead, Dobrochna encouraged me to investigate existing community programs.

Months earlier in the spring of 2023, at the suggestion of my cousin, himself a violinist living in Vancouver, I'd joined the Associated Chamber Music Players (ACMP), an international social network of amateur musicians who played together upon request. One July day the same year, I received a welcome email from a woman who identified herself as the "volunteer Toronto representative on the North American Outreach Council of ACMP." Sharing her wealth of knowledge in a ensuing conversation, I discovered multiple options open to me nearby.

A few weeks later, I registered for the Adult Chamber Music Program run by University Settlement House, which offered courses for musicians at all levels wishing to play in small ensembles. Enrolling as an intermediate, I held my breath, waiting to find out with whom I'd be placed for eight weeks.

I also contacted Julian Fisher, director of the Toronto School for Strings Orchestra, to explore the possibility of joining his weekly program for amateur players. Recognizing I was falling back into my overambitious tendencies, I quickly opted out in favour of the chamber music program, with the hope I'd also perhaps participate in the string orchestra at a later date.

Then, in August, a somewhat intriguing and tantalizing email arrived in my inbox: "I found your name on the ACMP site. I know this is horribly short notice, but do you happen to be free tomorrow (Friday) afternoon to play Mendelssohn piano trios with a pianist visiting from Montreal? Unfortunately, he's returning to Montreal on Saturday morning so that's the only time that will work. We would be meeting at my house near Bathurst and Dupont. Here's hoping!"

A dream come true! I was being asked to play with other musicians!

Dobrochna was in Poland. What should I do? Accept and risk the embarrassment of being a drag on the other musicians? Politely bow out with some excuse in order not to potentially ruin my reputation for any further offers? As luck had it, I wasn't available for the suggested date and time. Rather than offer an alternative, I declined but not without learning more from this ACMP member about casual meet-ups to play in the neighbourhood.

This opportunity highlighted my need for some preparation and coaching in a program before feeling confident enough to play with others. Yet I felt convinced that day wouldn't be far off. And the thought of playing with others filled me with excitement.

That night, curling up in bed against Lawlor, I once again reflected on my decision to take up the cello. Earlier that day, waiting for a traffic light to change at the busy intersection of Spadina and College near my office, I'd bumped into an old acquaintance I hadn't seen in many years. Reconstructing our lives in a brief exchange of catch-up, I mentioned my involvement with the cello.

"You gotta be kidding?" Allison chirped in disbelief as if I'd told her I was taking a course on flight navigation to the moon.

"Yes," I repeated succinctly. "I've now been playing the cello for more than five years and I'm loving it." To save any further displays of incredulity on her part, I withheld the dramatic details of my accident, which had actually subtracted six months from my music studies.

My conversation with Allison reminded me of the one with my mother whose initial reaction to my musings about taking up the cello was: "Whatever possessed you to take up the cello?"

In the beginning, it wasn't unusual for my friends and colleagues to question my choice: "Why music now? Did you play an instrument before? Do you have a teacher? How did you find one? Can you read sheet music?" The question

I'd really sidestepped and wasn't sure I could answer was: "What did the cello mean to me and why its importance at this time?"

It was that question, insistent and persistent, intruding once again on my thoughts, that I was wrestling with for my own clarification.

Maybe it was about finding a new passion, a meaningful interest. Perhaps it was about retrieving a creative force that could sustain me through a period of life when so many of my friends were grappling with endings and losses. Loss of health, loss of work, loss of image and appearance, loss of abilities — the list went on and on. Maybe I'd decided to beat the odds on *my* terms. I was going to find something that could invite the life force once again into my being in a way I hadn't encountered before. Or at least I hoped it would.

My friend, Ann, a compulsively avid reader, once sent me some articles on *duende*, the Spanish concept of magical power that could inhabit one's being in times of artistic creation and performance. I thought of *duende* as inspired performance, when we are overtaken by an inexpressible force. Yet it is also a struggle against obstacles and outside forces, untoward circumstances and impediments.

That evening, I thought about one of the articles so beautifully penned by the Spanish poet Federico García Lorca on the *duende*. He'd beautifully written, here recalled with my imprecise memory, that *duende* was a force, not a labour, a struggle, not a thought. It wasn't about the muses that dictated or the angels that dazzled. Rather it was a struggle to be aroused, to be possessed, to feel the life force in one's veins surging up, "inside, from the soles of the feet."

Maybe the answer lay in that word *possessed*. Perhaps I wanted to be overtaken by something new, novel, potentially life-enhancing. Wasn't that what Lorca was trying to state when he wrote: "Struggle with *duende*." To be taken over, to give oneself up to something fully in total abandonment?

One day at the end of the summer, I retreated to my practice space and listened once again to the musical genius of Yo-Yo Ma playing the *largo* movement from Dvořák's *New World Symphony* (also referred to as *Going Home*). Astronaut Neil Armstrong brought a tape of this symphony with him on the *Apollo 11* mission to the moon. It had been performed and recorded during the height of the Covid epidemic, a time of global suffering and hardship. With its lyricism and melodic lines, Yo-Yo wrote that he felt it would provide others with a soothing balm of comfort.

At Dobrochna's suggestion, I'd memorized this short section of the movement with its simple tune and repetitive notes. Holding Simone in my arm's embrace, I placed my bow firmly on the strings, closed my eyes, and inhaled and exhaled deeply with intention. Listening to the first few bars silently inside, now fully prepared, I gently slid my bow across the strings. Without interruption, I played *Going Home* from beginning to end. With tears streaming down my cheeks, I felt pleased and satisfied by my improvisation. For a few precious moments, I was *in the flow*, connected to my heart in a state of transcendence.

Notes

Chapter Four: Relationships

1. Alvin C. White, *The Strad* 31, no. 363 (July 1920), reproduced in *The Strad* 131 (July 2020), 89.

Chapter Eight: First House Concert

1. Stephen Hough, *Rough Ideas: Reflections on Music and More* (New York: Picador/Farrar, Straus and Giroux, 2020), 17.

Chapter Ten: Practise, Practise!

1. "9 Ways to Develop a Flexible Bow Hold," *The Strad*, February 16, 2023. Reprints of comments by Arthur Broadley from *The Strad*, October 1905, and Simon Fischler, December 2005, thestrad. com/playing-hub/9-ways-to-develop-a-flexible-bow-hold/6747. article?adredir=1.

2. Alan Rusbridger, *Play It Again: An Amateur Against the Impossible* (New York: Farrar, Straus and Giroux, 2013), 57.

3. Hough, *Rough Ideas*, 135.

Chapter Eleven: Age and Aging

1. Sam Zygmuntowicz, "Late ... but Worth the Wait," *The Strad* 131 (December 2020), 24, digitaleditions.thestrad.com/magazine/reader/206878?pageNumber=25.

2. Pablo Casals, *Joys and Sorrows* (New York: Simon & Schuster, 1974), 15.

3. See Rich Karlgaard, *Late Bloomers: The Hidden Strengths of Learning and Succeeding at Your Own Pace* (New York: Crown, 2021).

4. See Ari L. Goldman, *The Late Starters Orchestra* (Chapel Hill, NC: Algonquin Books, 2014).

5. See Malcolm Gladwell, *Outliers: The Story of Success* (Boston: Little, Brown, 2008).

6. See Nell Painter, *Old in Art School: A Memoir of Starting Over* (New York: Counterpoint Press, 2018).

Chapter Twelve: The Search for a New Cello

1. See Helena Attlee, *Lev's Violin: An Italian Adventure* (New York: Penguin, 2022).

Chapter Thirteen: The Nature of Music

1. Anthony Storr, *Music and the Mind* (New York: Maxwell Macmillan, 1992). 126. Storr paraphrases this idea from Plato's *The Republic*.

2. Nicholas Kenyon, *The Life of Music: New Adventures in the Western Classical Tradition* (New Haven, CT: Yale University Press, 2021), 19, 22. Kenyon discusses Plato's views on music's power.

3. Storr, *Music and the Mind*.

4. For the 1973 Leonard Bernstein *The Unanswered Question* lectures, see openculture.com/2012/03/leonard_bernsteins_masterful_lectures_on_music.html.

Chapter Fourteen: Billy

1. See Oliver Sachs, *Musicophilia: Tales of Music and the Brain* (Toronto: Vintage Canada, 2008); Daniel J. Levitin, *This Is Your Brain on Music: The Science of a Human Obsession* (New York: Plume, 2006); and Aniruddh D. Patel, *Music, Language, and the Brain* (New York: Oxford University Press, 2010).

Chapter Fifteen: Duets

1. See Eric Siblin, *The Cello Suites: J.S. Bach, Pablo Casals, and the Search for a Baroque Masterpiece* (Toronto: House of Anansi, 2010).

2. See Philip Ball, *The Music Instinct: How Music Works and Why We Can't Do Without It* (New York: Oxford University Press, 2010; Alex Ross, *Listen to This* (New York: Farrar, Straus & Giroux, 2010); and Philip Glass, *Words Without Music: A Memoir* (New York: Liveright, 2015).

Chapter Seventeen: Exploring Simone's Roots

1. Suzanne Simard, *Finding the Mother Tree: Discovering the Wisdom of the Forest* (Toronto: Allen Lane Canada, 2021), 283.

2. David Abram, *Becoming Animal: An Earthly Cosmology* (New York: Pantheon, 2010), 192.

3. Simard, *Finding the Mother Tree*, 294.

4. Stefano Scarampella (1843–1924) was one of the more modern Italian violin makers whose name has made it into the ranks of the illustrious few for the quality of their work.

Suggested Reading

My musical journey was enhanced and enriched by many books. Some were recommended by others and some I stumbled across quite serendipitously. These book suggestions reflect my taste but may be of interest to readers.

Memoirs

Attlee, Helena. *Lev's Violin: A Story of Music, Culture, and Italian Adventure*. New York: Penguin, 2022.

Barenboim, Daniel. *Everything Is Connected: The Power of Music*. London: Weidenfeld & Nicolson, 2008.

Casals, Pablo. *Joys and Sorrows*. New York: Simon & Schuster, 1974.

Delbanco, Nicholas. *The Countess of Stanlein Restored: A History of the Countess of Stanlein Ex Paganini Stradivarius Cello of 1707*. London: Verso Books, 2001.

Glass, Philip. *Words Without Music: A Memoir*. New York: Liveright, 2015.

Holt, John Caldwell. *Never Too Late: My Musical Life Story*. New York: Delacorte, 1978.

Horvath, Janet. *The Cello Still Sings: A Generational Story of the Holocaust and the Transformative Power of Music*. Amsterdam: Amsterdam Publishers, 2023.

Painter, Nell. *Old in Art School: A Memoir of Starting Over*. New York: Counterpoint Press, 2018.

Prieto, Carlos. *The Adventures of a Cello*. Austin, TX: University of Texas Press, 2006.

Rusbridger, Alan. *Play It Again: An Amateur Against the Impossible.* London: Vintage Books, 2014.

Steinhardt, Arnold. *Indivisible by Four: A String Quartet in Pursuit of Harmony.* New York: Farrar, Straus & Giroux, 1998.

Wilson, Miranda. *The Well-Tempered Cello: Life with Bach's Cello Suites.* Washington, DC: Fairhaven Press, 2022.

Music Appreciation

Ball, Philip. *The Music Instinct: How Music Works and Why We Can't Do Without It.* New York: Oxford University Press, 2010.

Copland, Aaron. *What to Listen for in Music.* New York: Signet Classics, 2002.

Goldman, Ari L. *The Late Starters Orchestra.* Chapel Hill, NC: Algonquin Books, 2014.

Hodges, Natalie. *Uncommon Measure: A Journey Through Music, Performance and the Science of Time.* New York: Bellevue Literary Press, 2022.

Hough, Stephen. *Rough Ideas: Reflections on Music and More.* New York: Farrar, Straus & Giroux, 2020.

Isserlis, Steven. *The Bach Cello Suites: A Companion.* London: Faber & Faber, 2021.

____. *Robert Schumann's Advice to Young Musicians: Revisited by Steven Isserlis.* London: Faber & Faber, 2016.

Kapilow, Rob. *All You Have to Do Is Listen: Music from the Inside Out.* Hoboken, NJ: John Wiley & Sons, 2008.

Kenyon, Nicholas. *The Life of Music: New Adventures in the Western Classical Tradition.* New Haven, CT: Yale University Press, 2021.

Pleeth, William. *Cello.* Yehudi Menuhin Music Guides. London: Kahn & Averill, 1992.

Ross, Alex. *Listen to This.* New York: Farrar, Straus & Giroux, 2010.

____. *The Rest Is Noise: Listening to the Twentieth Century.* New York: Picador, 2008.

Siblin, Eric. *The Cello Suites: J.S. Bach, Pablo Casals and the Search for a Baroque Masterpiece*. Toronto: House of Anansi, 2010.

Storr, Anthony. *Music and the Mind*. New York: Maxwell Macmillan, 1992.

Suzuki, Shinichi. *Nurtured by Love: The Classic Approach to Talent Education*. Athens, OH: Senzay Publications, 1983.

Vulliamy, Ed. *When Words Fail: A Life with Music, War and Peace*. London: Granta, 2018.

Wilson, Elizabeth. *Jacqueline du Pré*. London: Weidenfeld & Nicolson, 1998.

Acknowledgements

Writing about a musical journey in later life might have remained an interesting notion had it not been for the encouragement and support of many friends and music lovers. First, I would like to thank my cello teacher, Dobrochna Zubek, who took me seriously from our first encounter and never let me falter when I questioned or doubted my musical pursuit. Second, I would like to express my deep gratitude to Lois Schklar, my writing buddy, who listened to me read aloud rambling fragments of early drafts and never failed to encourage me to complete this writing project.

Many musicians — composers, performers, and luthiers — have had input into the background research and I would like to thank all of them for their important input. In particular, these include my conversations with Joseph Johnson, Rachel Mercer, Norbert Palej, Itzel Avila, Michelle Ashley, Ric Heinl, and my recently discovered second cousin, Keith Lawrence.

I am grateful to Brian Gable for the wonderfully delightful sketches that illustrate the chapters. His immediate and positive response was well appreciated. I would also like to thank the readers and editors who have had invaluable input into the final product of this book, notably Jane Warren, Steven Beattie, and especially Michael Carroll, for his ever-present optimism, invaluable editorial assistance, and publishing advice. I would also like to thank Daniel Crack for his wonderful design and production work on my book.

Finally, I wish to thank Lawlor, my husband and soulmate, who has stood by me in all times, whether of crisis or calm, light or darkness.